Contents

Preface

Peering from beneath his mistress Margie's blond curls, Beanie sniffed at me from atop his eye-level perch with the same inquisitiveness I had for him. Satisfied that I was neither dangerous nor edible, Beanie resumed his exploration of Margie's ear. Whiskers twitching like hummingbird wings, he gave a lick to her cheek and headed around the nape of her neck. She reached around and, cupping him in her hand, gently lifted him until he released his grasp and returned him to his brother Cecil, waiting in a large glass aquarium. With no less enthusiasm than a dog shows when receiving a biscuit, Beanie and Cecil took the bits of marshmallow Margie offered. Pure white with red eyes and generous in proportion, these rats were bred for a research project to study obesity, Margie explains. Now they're content to share the Cambridge apartment of a graduate student.

This was my introduction to pet rats. I believe the scenario explains well the answer to the question "Why would anyone want one, anyway?" Affectionate, intelligent, and easy to care for, rats are ideal companions for busy, apartment-dwelling people. Anyone who looks beyond the reputation of rats as destructive, verminous creatures will see them as industrious survivors with admirable ability to adapt. More than any other small rodent, pet rats learn to trust humans and seem to seek out our companionship. People who have kept more than one rat are quick to point out that each has a unique personality that it expresses in its habits and antics.

In my practice of veterinary medicine in California, exotic species were well represented in our group of clients. Often there was an ailing boa constrictor in one examination room, a sniffling rat in the next, and a recently purchased parrot in the third. While the owner of the boa constrictor might question the sanity of the rat owner, for bringing what logically represented dinner for his snake to the veterinarian, the rat owner would undoubtedly take offense. Grateful for the simple joy animals bring into our lives, most owners want to provide the best homes and care to their small and unusual friends in return.

That is the purpose of this book. It is my hope that the information I have written will answer many of the questions that you have about purchasing, breeding, husbandry, and diseases of domestic rats. I have tried to anticipate these questions based on inquiries made of me during examinations and on observations I have made about myths and misinformation perpetuated among rat fanciers. Because it is so important to have knowledge of their wild ancestors in order to understand and enjoy our domestic animals, I have included background information about wild rats whenever possible. Suggestions on how to make this text more useful to you are warmly welcome.

Caro___ _____, D.V.M.

Rats

All about Selection, Husbandry,
Nutrition, Breeding and Diseases.
With a Special Chapter on Understanding Rats.

Color Photograph by Karin Skogstad;
Illustrations by Fritz W. Köhler and Michele Earle-Bridges

All inquires should be addressed to:
Barron's Educational Series, Inc.
250 Wireless Boulevard
Hauppauge, NY 11788

International Standard Book No. 0-8120-4535-1

Library of Congress Catalog Card No. 91-15061

Library of Congress Cataloging-in-Publication Data

Himsel, Carol A.
   Rats: all about selection, husbandry, nutrition, breeding, and diseases, with a special chapter on understanding rats/ Carol A. Himsel; with color photographs by Karin Skogstad and illustrations by Fritz W. Köhler and Michele Earle-Bridges.
     p. cm.
   Includes bibliographical references and index.
   ISBN 0-8120-4535-1
   1. Rats as pets. I. Title.
SF459.R3H56 1991
636'.93233 — dc20   91-15061
                                     CIP

Printed in Hong Kong

5 6 7 8 9   4900   13 12 11 10 9 8

About the Author:
After practicing for several years in northern California, Dr. Carol Himsel currently resides in rural Connecticut where she practices veterinary medicine and surgery for small companion animals and llamas. In addition, Dr. Himsel is a veterinary consultant and has written research and clinical articles for the scientific community. When she is not caring for other peoples' animals, Dr. Himsel spends her time caring for Willie, Neige, Cocoa and Molly and dabbles in the arts of photography and cooking.

Note of Warning
There are a few diseases of domestic rats that can be transmitted to humans (see page 65). If your rat shows any sign of illness (see page 49), you should definitely call the veterinarian, and if you are at all worried that your own health might be affected, consult your doctor.
   Some people are allergic to animal hair. If you think you might have such an allergy, ask your doctor before bringing home a rat.

Preface

Acknowledgments

I am most grateful to several of my colleagues for their efforts in assisting me in preparation of this manuscript. First, many thanks is extended to Dr. Fredric Stevens of Vetsoft, Veterinary Software, without whose limitless patience and expertise in computers I would still be writing this manuscript on yellow legal paper. As most of this book was written in the evening after long hours in the veterinary hospital, Dr. Stevens gave generously of his time during moments of crisis, usually in the middle of the night, after the author had accidentally deleted large portions of the text.

I also wish to thank Dr. Fredric Frye for introducing me to the editors at Barron's and for his encouragement and devotion to my professional development over the last several years. Appreciation is given to Don Reis and the editors at Barron's for their direction and suggestions and efforts to acquire the fine photographs included in this book. I am also grateful to Dr. Helgard Niewisch for her enthusiastic review of the manuscript. And thanks, too, to James.

Carol A. Himsel, D.V.M.
Spring 1991

To Heidi

Understanding Rats

The Zoology of Rats

The group of animals that zoologists call rodents comprises almost forty percent of all mammals. By sheer numbers, these animals have been tremendously successful. But their success can also be measured by their diversity of form and ability to adapt to nearly every type of climate on this planet.

You may be quite surprised to learn just who your rat's relations are! Rodents have been divided into three groups based on the types of jaw muscles involved in gnawing. The first group, that of the squirrel-like rodents, includes nearly 380 species. Squirrels, marmots, beavers, gophers, and woodchucks all belong to this group. The oldest known fossil records of rodents, some 60 million years old, are from animals of this group that are now extinct.

A second group are the mouselike rodents. This is the largest collection, 1,082 species in all; it includes mice, hamsters, lemmings, and all kinds of rats. Guinea pigs, chinchillas, porcupines, and the biggest rodent, the capybara, all belong to the third group of animals called cavy-like rodents, of which there are about 190 species.

Common to these seemingly diverse groups of rodents is a characteristic bony jaw structure and associated muscles that give these animals the ability to gnaw through nearly everything. In fact, the word "rodent" is derived from the Latin *rodere,* which means "to gnaw." Rodents have four opposing incisors, two in the upper jaw and two in the lower. These teeth grow continuously throughout the animal's life, approximately 5 inches (12.5 cm) each year. A large space, called a di-

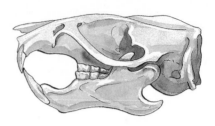

A space called a "diastema" lies between the front incisor teeth and rear molars on both sides of the rat's jaws.

astema, separates the incisor teeth from the grinding molars in the rear. The absence of canine teeth and premolars allows a rodent to draw its lips into the mouth behind the incisors. This effectively closes off the rest of the oral space as the animal gnaws its way along.

The tremendous success of rodents as a whole is largely attributable to their lack of specialization. They are resourceful consumers, capable of handling a wide variety of foods. All rodents are omnivorous and can adapt their diet to whatever food is available. Some species have adapted to environments with little water. The most successful of all rodents, rats and mice, live close enough to humans to partake of their bounty and find shelter in their dwellings. Others have evolved physiologic mechanisms that allow them to live in climates with extreme temperatures.

Their prolific nature has resulted in rapid selection of traits that permit rodents to thrive, not just survive.

As a rat fancier, you are a member of a small but growing number of people who recognize these animals as delightful companions. Over many centuries, rats have earned the reputations of being highly destructive carriers and transmitters of disease. They destroy dwellings, crops, and stored food; and they spread disease through their urine and feces, through bite wounds, and by acting as hosts to disease-carrying fleas.

Accurate information about the current population densities of the two major species of rats is not available. Species distribution and numbers were studied earlier in the twentieth century when scientists were learning about ways to eliminate wild rats. What these scientists learned was that rat population numbers depended upon two factors: food supply and harborage. Predictably, rats are prevalent in areas that have poor sanitation, careless disposal of garbage, and easy access to stored food. Rats are more often found in warmer climates, and unless a building is specifically "rat-proofed," they will enter it looking for food and shelter.

"Rat-proof" construction is designed to eliminate a rat's access to a building by inhibiting its ability to gnaw, burrow, climb, or squeeze through a $1/2$-inch (1.3 cm) opening. Channels made of materials difficult for a rat to gnaw are placed below doors, at the height of a standard rat sitting on its haunches, the position a rat assumes to do its gnawing. Stud boards and interior nails are spaced 18 inches (46 cm) apart so that they can't be reached by most rats. L-shaped curtain walls extending below the foundation discourage burrowing under buildings. Openings where wires and pipes enter walls are fitted with rat guards.

Despite such efforts, wild rats are still found inside human dwellings. Their powerful jaw muscles enable them to chew through lead, uncured concrete, and adobe brick, not to

Rats sit upright on their haunches when gnawing through storage containers or walls. "Rat-height" channels below doors, made of materials that are difficult for rats to gnaw, discourage them from entering buildings.

mention the easy stuff like cardboard and burlap. Aside from the direct destruction, rats contaminate food with their urine, droppings and hair, making the food unfit for consumption.

Historically, rats have been directly or indirectly responsible for the deaths of millions of people, largely because of the disease bubonic plague. During the fourteenth century, three major epidemics of plague swept across Europe. Bubonic plague, caused by the bacteria *Yersinia pestis* is highly fatal to rats, too. People became ill and died in massive numbers when they came in contact with rat carcasses or were bitten by rat fleas carrying the bacteria. Remember that sanitation, as we know it, was almost nonexistent at the time, and taking baths was considered unhealthy. Rats flourished in the garbage and sewage thrown into the streets.

Around the world, cases of bubonic plague continue to occur, even in modern, industrial-

Understanding Rats

Physical characteristics of wild rats

	Rattus norvegicus	*Rattus rattus*
Weight	10–17 oz (280–480 gm)	4–12 oz (115–280 gm)
Length	12–18 in (32–46 cm)	14–18 in (35–46 cm)
Body Shape	chubby	slender
Muzzle	short	elongated
Ears	less than ³/₄ in, (2 cm) covered by fine hairs	more than ³/₄ in (2 cm), hairless
Tail	shorter than length of body and head combined	longer than length of body and head combined

R. norvegicus, R. rattus. Zoologists use body weight and other physical characteristics to classify rats into different species. The table above lists differences between the two most common species of wild rats.

ized societies. And there are a few other bacteria and viruses that scientists know are transmissible from wild rats to humans. Still other disease agents are theoretically transmissible, but their real threat is unknown. One example of a bacterial disease transmitted by wild rats is leptospirosis. *Leptospira* germs are harbored by wild rodents and transmitted primarily to livestock through drinking water contaminated with rat urine. In farm animals and humans, leptospirosis results in liver, kidney, and reproductive diseases.

It should be emphasized, lest you are left looking in horror at your pet rat, that the description of the relationship between rats and humans given earlier pertains to populations of wild rats, not the domesticated variety. With selective breeding and better sanitation and husbandry practices, domestic rats have become less aggressive, more accustomed to confinement, and free from dangerous diseases carried by their wild counterparts.

The Nature of Rats

The mouselike rodents, which include rats, probably originated in the Southeast Asian islands, India, central Asia, and China before the Ice Age. When the shipping trade with people in this part of the world began, so did

Understanding Rats

the worldwide distribution of rats. First to invade Europe was the black, or roof, rat, *Rattus rattus*. This was around the twelfth century. The larger and more aggressive brown rat, *Rattus norvegicus,* came several hundred years later, in the early eighteenth century. Within a hundred years, brown rats were established in America. The black rat had arrived in America much earlier, in the sixteenth century.

Besides these two, there are many other species of rats distributed around the world, possibly several hundred. None has influenced history and the human race to the same extent. In the United States and in most other countries, the two most important species of rats to share man's habitat remain *Rattus norvegicus* and *Rattus rattus*. Animals who live in close association with people and yet are not domesticated like livestock, dogs, and cats are termed "commensal," which means "eating at the same table." This word can certainly be applied to rats.

R. norvegicus and *R. rattus* animals can be distinguished by physical characteristics as well as by the way they behave—that is, where they are likely to be found geographically and by habitat. Rat-control officials and public health agents make use of these differences in eradication programs necessary to control populations of wild rats in urban and rural areas. Let's look at the physical differences first.

R. norvegicus, the likely granddaddy of the domestic pet rat, is the larger of the two species. It weighs between 10 and 17 ounces (280–480 gm) and ranges in length from 12 to a remarkable 18 inches (32–46 cm). Its body is round and tapers toward the neck. Its nose or

muzzle is relatively short and its ears are small, usually less than $^3/_4$ inch (2 cm) in length, and are covered with fine hairs. *R. norvegicus* has a tail that is usually shorter than the length of its head and body.

The roof rat, *R. rattus,* can also achieve lengths of 14 to 18 inches (35–46 cm). However, this rat is more slender than its cousin and weighs between 4 and 12 ounces (115–280 gm). Its nose is more elongated, and its ears are not covered with the same fine layer of hairs and are generally longer than $^3/_4$ inch (2 cm). This rat species has a tail that may be longer than the head and body together.

Characteristic Behavior Patterns

The brown rat may seem lumbering at potentially twice the body weight of the roof rat, but don't be fooled! Rats are wily and agile creatures, as rat-control officials are quick to mention. Despite their size, they can enter buildings and other spaces through openings no larger than a quarter. They can leap dis-

Rats have an excellent sense of balance. They can negotiate clotheslines and telephone cables with ease.

Understanding Rats

A threatened rat confronts an opponent by rearing up on its hind legs and uttering a cry that is too shrill to be heard by human ears.

The whiskers on the rat's face are very sensitive to touch.

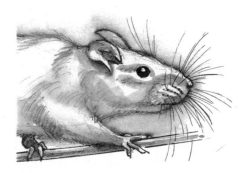

The sensitive whiskers compensate for the rat's poor vision.

tances of 8 feet from a standstill and heights of 2 to 3 feet. Like their arch enemy the cat, rats can fall from great distances and land unharmed on their feet.

Roof rats are considered to be better acrobats than their cousins, although brown rats are more fierce and will drive roof rats away. If they do share buildings, roof rats will likely be found above the ground floor, with brown rats closer to the basement and foundation. To reach such heights, a rat will take advantage of any surface on which it can get a toehold and will even scale a vertical wall. If the wall is smooth, a rat will brace its back against a parallel drainpipe. Inside walls, they will travel between nails and stud boards less than 18 inches apart. Rats will also use clotheslines and telephone lines as circus high wires to get from one place to another.

During warm months, brown rats will leave the protection of buildings and will migrate into the countryside to find plentiful food supplies on farms. In rural places these creatures will live in elaborate labyrinths of burrows with multiple entrances and exits. These habitats are usually no deeper than 18 inches underground. Sometimes roof rats will take over burrows abandoned by brown rats.

Special Senses

Of the five basic senses, the sense of sight is the least developed in rats. Although they are unable to see in great detail, rats do distinguish strongly contrasting shadows of light and dark. Rats do not see colors. They are good at judging distances and are quite accurate jumpers.

To compensate for poor vision, the sense of *touch* is very well-developed in rats. Free-roaming rats prefer to move along walls by using the vibrissae or whiskers on either side of the face. In addition, there are longer tactile hairs scattered over the body that help the rat to maneuver through burrows and other confined spaces.

Rats can taste about as well as humans, and they also have a strong attraction to sweets! Their sense of smell, however, is very keen and plays an enormously important role in reproduction and breeding, as we shall see. Rats can hear well, too. They respond more strongly to loud, sharp noises than to low, repetitive ones.

Obtaining a Rat

What Kind of Rat Is This?

Domestic rats, those used in research and kept as pets, were bred from the wild species *Rattus norvegicus*. These rats are commonly called by the names Norway, brown, and gray rat, or are named for the location where they are likely to be found: sewer rat, alley rat, wharf rat, etc.—hardly names you'd want to use to describe a creature that shares your home! More than likely, your rat is neither brown nor gray, nor did you entice it into your company from an alley downtown!

Earlier, we learned in which part of the world rats first appeared and how they spread into Europe and America. Now let's look at the rat's more recent history. About 100 years ago, scientists in Europe did entice free-living rats into their company, primarily for experiments in nutrition. Common people were keeping rats for sport even earlier in the 1800s. Hundreds of Norway rats were trapped and used for rat-baiting. For this game, rats were placed in a pit along with a ferocious terrier. Bets were placed on the dogs and the time it would take to kill every last rat. Rats with unusual pelts, particularly the albinos, were spared and used for breeding and shows. Some of these rats were given to scientists for experiments.

Around 1890 rats began to be used in scientific research in the United States. The origin of these rats is not clear. Some were brought by scientists from Europe coming to study in Philadelphia at the newly established Wistar Institute; others were probably wild-caught from the streets of the city itself. Prized for their prolific nature, rapid growth, small size, and willingness to accept human contact, rats

were sent to universities all over the country. With so many people now familiar with this creature, it's no wonder that a few made their way into homes as pets.

Variations in coat color and texture occur naturally in the rat population. The "standard" rat, *Rattus norvegicus,* has an agouti coat with a white or cream-colored underbelly. Agouti hairs are banded. Close inspection reveals that the hair shaft is striped by three colors: grayish blue next to the skin, yellow in the middle, and black on the tip. This banding pattern provides an excellent camouflage; nature has used it in many animal species, from Abyssinian cats to jackrabbits.

The variety in colors of rats is determined by modification of the rat's chromosomes. Chromosomes are packages of information inside every cell that determine such traits as how long the tail will grow, what color the eyes will be, and whether the hair will be curly or straight. Each one of these traits is carried on a specific place on the chromosome called a gene. Over time, the information carried in

Caring for a pair of rats is a good introduction to the responsibilities of pet ownership.

genes can change, or mutate. When this happens, offspring different from the parents emerge.

Why do genes mutate? No one really knows for sure. The sequence of events that takes place inside the cell to produce an egg and sperm is dizzyingly complex; it's a wonder that conception and birth ever occur at all.

Amidst all this deck shuffling, a few patterns have emerged that have resulted in several typical coat patterns and colors for rats. Two types of coat patterns are recognized: solid and spotted. Solid rats are found in a variety of colors: dark brown, black, chocolate, gray, lavender (very light gray, almost blue), lilac, yellow, sand, and silver. Albino rats of course, have no pigment at all.

Four types of spotted rats are recognized. Once again, the pattern of spots is determined by the genetic "library." The most commonly recognized pattern is called *hooded*, a term that aptly describes these pelts. Hooded rats have white bodies and dark heads and shoulders, with a stripe extending along the back. Similar to hooded rats is a variety called *notched*. In these rats, the hood is smaller and there is no dorsal stripe. *Irish* rats are white except for spots on the chest and belly.

A fourth pattern of spotting—*restricted*—is very rare and quite unlikely to occur in domestic pet rats, since purebred animals of this variety die soon after birth. Mixed-bred males of this type become sterile at around 3 months of age. *Restricted* rats are white except for limited color around the eyes and ears, although some closely resemble the hooded rat.

Color-pointed rats are known to occur, but they are not common. Called Himalayan rats,

these animals have dark noses and paws, like the cat variety of the same name. The dark pigmentation of the nose and paws is dependent on temperature: because the nose and paws are cooler, the fur in these areas grows in darker than the fur on the body, where the skin is warmer.

Some rats have naturally curly hair! Just as there are rex rabbits and rex cats, so there are *rex* varieties of rats. These animals have kinky, curly coats to one or more degrees. Genetic mutations have also produced rats with sparse hair coats, rats that are bald, and even some without whiskers.

Just about any physical or physiologic trait you can think of has been produced through serendipitous or careful breeding of rats. The differences in physical traits determined by the information on a gene are called phenotypes.

A Few Considerations Before Choosing a Rat

Who might consider adopting a rat? Rats are small and quiet. They never coax to be fed; they never howl during thunderstorms. They take up very little space and don't cost much to feed. In fact, they eat just about anything you do. And you never have to take them out for a walk in the rain. Rats don't need vaccinations or a license from the county. You can take them with you on vacation or ask a friend to look after them. Most landlords accept "small animals in cages" as tenants. Rats are even found as pets in college dormitories.

Rats are good companions for people who enjoy the company of animals but don't have a lot of time to devote to their care, socializa-

Obtaining a Rat

Mutual grooming strengthens the bonds between the members of the group.

tion, and training. The elderly and other shut-ins may enjoy looking after one or two because of their small size and the relative ease of cleaning the habitat. Classroom rats are an excellent learning tool. Children learn about nature, intelligence, and nutrition, as well as about the responsibility of caring for animals.

It is truly a privilege to be able to share our home with a pet. But it requires not only the initial expense of purchasing an animal but also the ongoing commitment of time and money to care for it properly. Too often veterinarians and humane society workers are asked to kill a pet because its owner has grown bored with it or unable to afford its care. If you have decided to buy or adopt a rat, please consider the following issues:

- Do you have the time each day to feed a rat nutritious foods, give it fresh water, and clean its habitat?
- Do you have the time each day to exercise and play with a rat?
- Do you have a readily available source of a balanced rodent diet?

- Do you have enough money to buy or build a safe habitat of adequate size? Do you have a place to put this habitat?
- Are all household members able to understand how to hold and play with a rat? Are some of the children too young to do this? Will the other pets at home accept a new arrival?
- What happens if your rat gets sick? Will you be willing to take it to the veterinarian, or are you more inclined to wait and see what will happen?
- Do you know a veterinarian who can take care of sick rats? Do you know how much it might cost for your rat to be examined?
- Who will care for your rat when you go on a trip?
- Did you know that rats can be destructive and leave droppings and urine on you and around the house?
- How will you feel when your rat dies?

These are questions that anyone who is thinking of adopting or buying a rat (or any pet) should answer. Discuss them openly with everyone in the household who might come in contact with or be affected by the animal. When they are answered to your satisfaction, you can get down to the business of finding your rat.

Where to Obtain a Pet Rat

Many pet stores keep rats in stock and sell them for two or three dollars. Pet-store rats are sold not only as pets but also as food for captive reptiles such as snakes and some carnivorous (meat-eating) lizards and birds. If your local pet store does not stock rats, it probably can order one specially for you. Un-

14

fortunately, this approach does not offer you the advantage of selecting a rat based on personality, coat, or some other trait.

Pet stores often purchase their rat stock from people in the community who keep one or more breeding pairs of rats as pets. Many of these private breeders advertise in the newspaper. These rats are frequently healthier than those available from a pet store, where the number of animals kept in confinement and the stress of constant scrutiny may predispose rats to disease.

You might inquire about obtaining a rat from a university colony that breeds rats for use in research. Usually, these rats are of the albino variety. Also check with the animal rescue shelter or humane society in your area. These organizations sometimes acquire unusual pets in need of homes.

Your veterinarian may be able to advise you of the best source in your area to obtain healthy rats.

Characteristics to Help You Choose

As a rule, you should adopt or buy a young rat, one that is approximately a month old. A young rat is much easier to socialize and tame than a mature one. You should bear this in mind especially if you are purchasing the rat at a pet store, since the store employees rarely have time to get the animals accustomed to handling by humans. A private rat breeder may handle the animals so often that they become accustomed to human touch and voice before adoption or purchase.

There is little difference between male and female rats with respect to learning ability and capacity for affection. Both sexes adapt quickly to being carried, stroked, and hand-fed. They are equally inquisitive and eager to explore any nook or cranny they encounter.

The sex of a rat is a consideration if you will be housing two or more rats. Mature male rats may fight with each other, sometimes aggressively enough to cause injury. This is more likely to occur if the habitat is too small for the number of animals it houses or if a mature female is kept in the males' company. Same-sex siblings or mixed pairs make much better companions. Be sure to provide a large enough enclosure if you plan to keep two or more rats together, and be prepared to provide separate quarters if your rats don't get along. Try to choose a rat that is active and friendly toward you. More than likely, a male and female will get along so nicely that you will soon see offspring.

The rat's pelt should be uniform, and free of bald spots, wounds, and flaky skin. It should not limp or hold a paw or leg abnormally while walking or sitting down. The corners of the eyes and the nostrils should be free of discharge or brownish-red discoloration. The rat's head should be held upright, not tipped to one side. Listen for any sneezing and look at the character of the droppings in the cage. They should be formed, not puddled in a corner. Once you are satisfied that you have found a healthy group of rats, the only task that remains is to choose the handsomest, smartest, most curious, and most affectionate rat of the bunch.

Are the habitats clean? Does the food and water look fresh? Inquire about the source of the rats, how long they have been at the pet store, and their approximate age. You should not purchase an animal that has been kept in a dirty cage or one that shows any signs of respiratory disease or diarrhea. Nor should you purchase a rat that has been housed with other sick animals. Poor husbandry predisposes the rat to diseases that may show up after you take it home.

If you already have a rat and want a companion for it, or if you want to introduce new breeding stock into your colony, every new rat you acquire should be isolated from the rats you currently own. Put the new rat or rats into a separate habitat so you can observe them for signs of disease. The new rats should be isolated for at least two weeks. If you purchase two new rats from the same pet store you don't need to put each one into its own cage or aquarium; one will suffice.

Transporting the rat to its new home can bring on illnesses that were incubating but not visible at the time you purchased it. Respiratory infections and conjunctivitis are common rat illnesses. If your new rat does show signs of illness, perform feeding and cleaning chores for the older rats first. After attending to the new rat, wash your hands thoroughly—especially if you will then be handling the older rats again. First consult your veterinarian and treat the sick animals. If *any* of your rats appears to be sick, don't allow it to mingle with the other rats—even after the isolation period.

These precautions can prevent the spread and minimize the severity of disease in a rat colony. Failure to follow these precautions can lead to rapid spread of an illness, just as cold germs spread through a classroom of children.

Rats groom by licking their fur and paws and rubbing their faces. Oil, produced by glands in the skin, is distributed over the coat and acts as waterproofing. ▶

Supplies and Housing

Kinds of Habitats

Unless you are directly supervising your rat's exploration and playtime, you should keep your friend in an escape-proof enclosure. You can buy rodent habitats at a pet store. Most people choose either a galvanized wire cage or glass aquarium. Both types of habitat have advantages and disadvantages, and they cost about the same.

Cages vary in size, shape, and number of tiers or levels connected by ladders or ramps. They are lightweight, and because they can be scrubbed with a brush, rinsed, and left to air-dry, they are easy to keep clean. Cages provide good ventilation so bedding stays drier and ammonia levels stay low. A cage is fairly escape-proof—provided its door is latched securely and the wires are close together.

But cages have negative aspects as well. Over time, the acids in the animals' urine corrodes cages. Furthermore, galvanized steel cages contain the metal zinc. Rats can become poisoned by the zinc if they lick or chew on the wires often. Scientists worry about zinc poisoning so much that they don't use wire cages for their animals.

Another problem with housing rats in cages is that the rats can develop large foot calluses climbing and standing on the wire surface. These calluses can become infected and painful sores. In addition a rat may get a leg caught

Minimum Cage Sizes for Rats	
Weight of rat — ounces (grams)	Floor area/rat — square inches (cm²)
Up to 3.2 (100 gm)	17 (10 cm²)
3.2–6.4 (100–200 gm)	23 (148 cm²)
6.4–9.6 (200–300 gm)	29 (187 cm²)
Over 9.6 (300 gm)	40 (258 cm²)
Minimum cage height = 7 inches (18 cm)	

between the wires of a cage; injury to the rat's skin and tendons—even a broken bone—may result.

To prevent these injuries, the cage floor should be lined with a removable piece of Plexiglas. A hardware store can cut a piece of Plexiglas to size for you. Plexiglas is superior to other materials because it's sturdy, easy to clean, and nontoxic. Wood floors soak up urine and are difficult to disinfect. Wood also splinters, and the slivers can find their way into your rat's feet. Your rat is likely to chew up a wood floor too. Cardboard floors tend to become mushy from urine, and this can promote the growth of germs.

For many reasons, a Plexiglas or glass aquarium is better for housing a pet rat. The smooth flooring is much easier on the rat's feet, and you don't have to worry about zinc poisoning. Pet stores sell wire tops for most standard size aquariums that prevent rats from escaping. Many of these tops clip onto the aquarium; if the one you buy doesn't, you will have to weigh it down with a brick or a rock.

◀ Top: An older albino shares an apple with a younger rat.

Bottom: An albino female teaches her offspring about apples. This hooded rat baby prefers to sit on its dinner. It was recently weaned from its mother's milk, judging by the still prominent nipples on the female.

Supplies and Housing

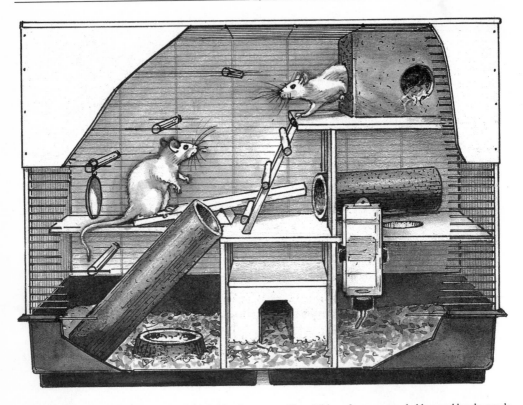

Either a wire cage or an aquarium is a suitable habitat for pet rats. The addition of toys, ramps, ladders, and levels guards against boredom and makes watching your rat more enjoyable.

Unfortunately, aquariums are heavy and can be cumbersome to move during cleaning. If you drop your aquarium, it may break. Although an aquarium's clear sides allow easy viewing of your pet, the ventilation in an aquarium is very limited. For that reason, you must make sure the aquarium is always clean. As bacteria grow in the soiled bedding, ammonia gas is produced and builds up inside the aquarium in high concentration. Ammonia gas irritates the rat's delicate respiratory tract, which can lead to severe and sometimes fatal pneumonia.

Plastic cages called Habitrails, which consist of a series of chambers connected by tunnels, are suitable for smaller rodents like hamsters and mice but are too small for an adult rat. You can build a cage or aquarium using your own design and materials. But make sure the habitat you build is sturdy enough to house a rat. Your rat can easily chew through a habitat made of wood, for example.

Supplies and Housing

Multilevel habitats may appear more interesting to you than the single-level variety. However, they may actually be more cramped once you add a food dish and several toys. I recommend that a habitat for a single rat be no smaller than a 33-quart aquarium. More animals need more space, so use common sense.

Bedding

Bedding material should provide warmth and absorb the rat's waste. An ideal bedding would be dust-free, absorbent, lightweight and free of harmful pesticides and resins. It would also be environmentally safe, inexpensive, and easily obtainable. Several bedding materials are available, none of which meets all these criteria.

The most commonly used bedding for rat habitats is sterilized cedar or pine wood shavings. Shavings are available at most pet stores in prepackaged and bulk form, sold by weight or volume. Some stores sell a processed corncob that is used for bedding. This material is more expensive than shavings and associated with a condition in young rats called "ringtail"; it should not be used in the habitats of nursing mothers and weanlings during dry winter months. Shredded newspaper is inexpensive and readily available; but it is not very absorbent, and the newsprint can get all over the fur. Recently, a superior cellulose material called Care Fresh (Absorption Corp.) has become available for use. It is a nontoxic, biodegradable, dust-free and absorbent paperlike product, but is not yet widely marketed. You can order it directly from the manufacturer by calling 1-800-242-2287; or you can ask your local pet store to stock it for you.

Food and Water Containers

To keep your rat's food free from urine and feces, put it into a crock, glass, or metal bowl. Plastic should not be used, because your rat will chew on the bowl and destroy it, possibly consuming small pieces in the process. Once a day, you should remove any fresh vegetables or fruits from the habitat so that they don't spoil and create a hazard to your rat's health. Your rat will probably hide choice morsels of food in the bedding, so check there as well.

Water should be provided in a sipper-tube bottle suspended by a rack from the side of the habitat. The water provided in this manner stays clean of bedding material and excrement, and doesn't spill easily. These bottles also prevent the water from evaporation, which is a handy feature if you have to leave your rat

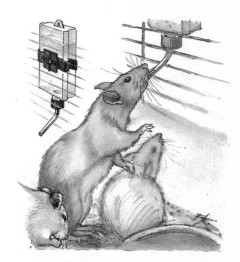

Hang a sipper-tube bottle from a rack on the side of the habitat to keep the rat's water clean. Be sure to tighten the cap securely before you turn it upside down!

alone for a day or two. A word of caution: always be sure to tighten the cap securely before you turn the bottle upside down!

Toys and Other Diversions

You will be your rat's major source of entertainment, but you can provide toys for the rat's amusement when you're not available. Small blocks of wood, smooth tree branches and cardboard tubes suitable for chewing, small boxes, wire wheels, and ramps are all good toys. (Make sure any wood blocks you provide are not treated with chemicals. Remember, a rat's teeth grow continuously, and the rat must grind them down by gnawing on objects and chewing food.) Use your imagination to design and build a maze with your rat's favorite food reward at the end. Then see how quickly your rat learns to negotiate the pattern.

Most rats enjoy swimming. If your pet does, you might provide it with a tub or tank where it can take an occasional dip. However, this should only be done with your constant supervision.

The Cost of a Rat and Supplies

A rat purchased from a pet store costs about two dollars. Plan to spend between $35 and $40 for a habitat. A wire cover for an aquarium

Rats are good swimmers. By offering your rat a pool of water, you provide an opportunity for exercise and for bathing. Don't leave your rat unsupervised in the túb.

costs between $10 and $20. A small crock food bowl, sipper bottle, and hanging rack will run about $10 to 15. Ongoing expenses include those for food and bedding material. If you buy in bulk, food and bedding will cost approximately five dollars a month. Altogether, the expense to set yourself up is about $65 if you buy all your supplies new. You can pare down those costs by searching through the classified ads in your local paper for used pet supplies or by checking garage sales and tag sales.

Caring for Rats

Setting up Housekeeping

The type and size of your rat's habitat, the bedding and sanitation, the number of animals you house together and the way you feed them are all part of what is collectively termed husbandry. The health and longevity of your rats is directly related to the quality of your husbandry and nutrition. Close, cramped quarters, dirty bedding, drafts, excessive noise and lights, and spoiled food are stress factors that predispose all animals to disease. The subject of nutrition is discussed at some length in another section of this book. Here we will examine good husbandry practices that minimize the effects of environmental stressors.

The optimal habitat temperature for rats is between 65 to 80 degrees. The cage or aquarium should be located away from open windows and other spots where subject to drafts or direct sunlight, which can cause drastic temperature changes throughout the day.

If you hand-feed your rat most or all of its food, it will learn to trust you very quickly. Eventually, a food reward will no longer be necessary for you to pick it up and pet it.

The lighting in the habitat should be dim to moderate. Too much light can cause damage to the retina, or light-sensitive tissue at the back of the eyes. This is especially true of albino rats, which lack pigment in the iris. The iris is the colored part of the eye with a hole in the center called the pupil. In bright light, the pupil gets smaller to block out the intense light from reaching the retina. The retina is also protected by the pigment in the iris, which acts like built-in sunglasses.

Relative humidity in the rat's habitat should be maintained between 40 and 70 percent. Dry air is damaging to the rats respiratory tract, and is responsible for the condition ringtail. Health problems attributable to low humidity are usually seen in the winter months, when the air is naturally dry. This is made worse by the drying effects of your furnace and some bedding materials, particularly processed corncob—all rob the air of moisture and contribute to these health problems.

Starting Off on the Right Foot

You should have everything ready and in place when you bring your rat home for the first time. At first, place the habitat in a spot that is away from the center of activity. Later, when your rat is accustomed to the environment and to being handled, you can move the habitat to a busier part of the house if that is appropriate.

It's a good idea not to handle a new rat too much the first day. The new sights, sounds, and smells can be frightening to the rat. In the wild, rats eat, sleep and reproduce over quite a small territory, although they travel long distances for food if necessary. Allow your rat to explore, rearrange, and mark its new home with urine for most of the first day. Watch his exploration and speak softly until the rat becomes familiar with your voice.

After a short time, you can begin to put your hand into the habitat for your rat to sniff. Most likely, the rat will scurry to the other side of the habitat rather than approach you. If you offer small tidbits of food, the rat will learn that your presence promises something tasty and good. You will gain your rat's trust much more quickly if you feed it exclusively by hand.

How to Pick up a Rat

Eventually, your rat won't run away from your hand, but toward it! This action is motivated by the promise of food, of course, so give your rat its reward.

To pick up the rat, slide your hand under its belly. Of course the rat may not be content to sit idly in your palm and may crawl out of your hand and along your arm heading for your shoulder or folds in your clothes. Another possibility is that it will try to escape from the cage. Be prepared for either occurrence.

If your goal is to make friends, don't pick up your rat by the tail! When suspended in midair this way, a rat will paddle its feet and twist its body in an attempt to find solid footing. A very young rat or one unaccustomed to being handled may, out of panic and fear, try to bite you.

Occasionally it will be necessary to immobilize your rat—to give medication or to make an examination, for example. To do this, gather up the loose skin behind the back of the neck (called the "scruff") between your thumb and forefinger, and suspend the rat upright and cradled in your hand. A very trusting little rat

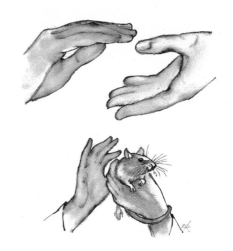

Rats should never be caught or lifted up by their tails. Instead, put your hand underneath the rat and hold it in the palm of your hand.

will most likely lie there without struggling; if it does give you a fight you may have to hold the back feet.

Housekeeping

An untidy habitat can lead to severe health problems for the rats, and odors that are unpleasant for you. How frequently you should clean the cage or aquarium depends on how messy your rat is with its food, the type of bedding used, the number of rats in the habitat, and the amount of waste that is produced.

If you have only one rat, all the bedding should be removed and the habitat scrubbed clean and rinsed about once a week. In between cleanings, remove the wet bedding and replace it with fresh bedding material as needed. Food and water containers should be emptied and thoroughly cleaned every day. Don't add vitamin supplements or other substances to the drinking water unless they have been specifically prescribed by your veterinarian. Vitamins added to water promote the growth of bacteria in the bottles.

Some abrasives and cleaners cause plastic and Plexiglas to turn cloudy. Even worse, some household cleaning products can be very toxic to rats. Residues in the cage or aquarium can vaporize and cause damage to a rat's internal organs and respiratory tract. So be sure to rinse all traces of cleaners from the surfaces of the habitat. A diluted bleach solution (3 percent) makes an excellent, inexpensive disinfectant.

Rats and Cats, and Other Combinations

Not everyone or every creature in your household will enjoy your pet rat in the same way you do. Cats and dogs are natural predators of rats and should not be left unsupervised in the presence of your rat when it is outside of its habitat. The same advice holds for hungry snakes.

Small children naturally take to animals. To many of them, rats are simply curious, furry bundles that feel nice against the skin. I have had many a teary child bring me an ailing rat. Very young children may not realize that rough handling can injure a rat or provoke it to bite. And, of course, there are children who intentionally mistreat small animals. Be sure to discuss how to handle and play with a rat with the little people in your household.

Rats are not domesticated to anywhere near the degree that other companion animals are. The more you interact with your rat, the more trusting and tame it will become. Eventually

To restrain your rat for examination or medication, grasp the loose skin behind its ears, between your thumb and forefinger. Some rats must first be wrapped in a small towel, leaving the head and neck exposed. Hold its rear feet with your fingers or up against your body.

you may find your rat curled up on your shoulder or in your pocket while you read.

Home on the Range

By nature, rats are explorers, gnawing their way through life. They cannot distinguish your expensive athletic shoes from the cardboard tube left in their cage as a toy. It is impossible to discipline a rat to leave wires, furniture or valuables alone. To prevent damage to your house and loss or injury of your rat, don't allow it to freely roam his environment, no matter how innocent and peaceful it appears perched up on your bookshelf.

Of course your rat can itself be injured if left to roam outside its enclosure. Here is a list of possible hazards:
- drafts
- excessive sunlight

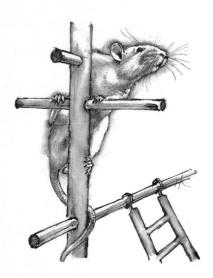

The rat uses its tail for balance and touch. Notice how it wraps its tail around your wrist or a perch inside the habitat, to keep from falling off.

To prevent injury or accidents, always supervise your rat when it is out of the habitat.

- other aggressive pets
- falling from heights
- falling objects
- open doors and windows
- electrical cords and outlets
- cleaning agents and other chemicals
- drugs in the medicine cabinet
- pesticides and herbicides
- alcoholic beverages
- caffeine
- recliners and convertible furniture
- trapping inside clothes dryers, refrigerators
- mousetraps
- sharp objects in trash
- rancid garbage
- automobile exhaust fumes
- unventilated cars on hot days
- plastic bags
- being stepped upon
- swinging doors
- toilets, other containers with water
- wood stoves and fireplaces
- portable heaters
- some houseplants (e.g., philodendrons)

Transporting Your Rat

From time to time, it may be necessary for you to take your rat on a brief excursion, outside the home—to the veterinary hospital, to a friend's house, or to a classroom, for example. For a few dollars, you can purchase a small rodent carrier made of clear, easy-to-clean plastic, with a vented top and handle. There's not much room inside one of these carriers, so don't plan on using one for a long trip. A shoe box with airholes also works fine as a carrier. Make sure the holes are not so large that your rat can squeeze through and

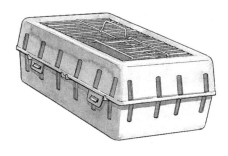

For long trips, a cat carrier is a must. These plastic carriers are inexpensive, easy to keep clean, and difficult for a rat to chew through. This one fits under the seat of an airplane.

escape, and use some string or tape to keep the lid in place. I've had a few patients come to the hospital inside a large brown grocery bag, too.

Longer trips require more preparation if you plan to bring along your rat—a move to another apartment or house or an extended vacation, for instance. If you are traveling by car, your only concern is how your rat will be received by the hotel wherever you are staying. If you are traveling by air or rail, you should inquire about the policy for transporting pets. Most airlines and railroads allow small animals in the cabin, provided the carrier fits under the seat in front of you. There is usually a limit of one animal in the cabin per flight.

On long trips, you can transport a rat directly in its habitat. If this is not practical, a cat carrier equipped with a handle and wire door may serve your purposes. Be sure to bring along plenty of bedding and food for your entire trip, unless you know that there will be a place to purchase these supplies at your destination. In essence, your rat will need its own suitcase!

Remember that during the summer months the inside of your car can become as hot as an oven in a very short time, even with a window cracked open. Never leave your rat or any other animal in a closed car in hot weather. If you are traveling in the winter time, take your rat with you when you leave the car. Hypothermia is just as deadly as overheating.

What About Your Vacation?

One of the nice things about having a pet rat is that you can leave it unattended while you go away on a short trip. Just be sure to provide enough food and fresh water for the number of days you will be gone. It may be necessary to hang a second sipper-tube bottle on the cage.

If you must leave home for longer than a couple of days, you should make arrangements for your rat to be cared for in your absence. Perhaps a friend would be willing to look after your rat in their home for this time. If this is not possible, consider contacting a boarding facility for animals. The facility probably has few requests for rat-sitting services and may be willing to look after your unusual pet—for a fee, of course. Some veterinary hospitals provide this service too, or have staff members who look after pets at home.

If you decide that you'd rather take your rat with you, consider the stresses involved for the rat. You may conclude that even a new environment and having a stranger provide its care is far less stressful for your rat. Still, I know of one rat, "Winnie," who spent a delightful time visiting the national parks in Colorado, Utah, and Nevada with her mistress, and camped in a tent the whole time!

Reproduction and Breeding

Initial Considerations

Wherever you decide to obtain your rat, you may be faced with the dilemma of choosing between two or more rats that are appealing in pelt and personality. If your circumstances allow you to have more than one animal, by all means, go ahead. Should you choose animals of both sexes, you may soon find yourself well-stocked with rats.

Instinctively, rats are polygamous, that is, they breed with more than one other rat during their lifetime. In artificial settings such as laboratories and breeding colonies, several breeding schemes are used to produce offspring with desired genetic traits. Rats may be inbred, which produces traits useful for specific experimental purposes. Or they may be outbred, which produces stock with variable and unpredictable characteristics.

Inbred rat colonies are produced by allowing closely related animals to mate. Because rats mature quickly, are capable of reproduc-

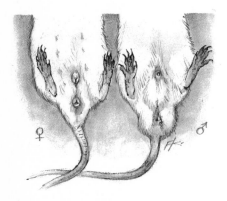

The distance between the anus and the genital papilla is smaller in females than in males. As they mature, males will develop a prominent scrotum containing the testicles, below the anus.

ing at an early age, and have a short gestation period, this can quickly result in fairly predictable physical and physiological characteristics in the majority if not all the offspring. This predictability is very important for some scientific experiments. Inbreeding also allows for the development of coat patterns and personalities pleasing to the rat fancier. This, in fact, may be your motivation in breeding rats.

Unfortunately, highly inbred animals, whether they be rats, cats or livestock, lack the quality of *hybrid vigor* common in animals that are more genetically varied. That is, they lack the stamina, longevity, resistance to disease, and physiologic adaptability that allows a species to thrive. So, along with the more desirable traits that breeders of animals strive to achieve, inbred rats exhibit a greater susceptibility to cancers and infectious diseases. Thus they have shorter lifespans.

That's why it is to the rat's advantage that it is polygamous. Unless you are planning to breed for a type of coat color or texture, you should not allow closely related rats in your colony to reproduce. This will maintain hybrid vigor in offspring.

Before embarking on a breeding project, be sure you make the necessary arrangements for care of the offspring. It is safe to assume that not all of your friends would appreciate the gift of a pet rat. Also keep in mind that baby rats sold to pet stores are likely to be resold as food for snakes and other carnivorous reptiles.

Sexing Rats

Determining the sex of a rat is best done through comparison with a litter or cage mate. Pick each one up and inspect the rats under the tails until you find two different configurations of anatomy. Males that have reached puberty have a prominent scrotum containing the testicles. When frightened or cold, male rats are capable of retracting the testicles into the body cavity. Below the scrotum is a distinctive genital papilla. Above the scrotum lies the anus. Female rats do not have a scrotum and the distance between the anus and external genitalia is shorter. The external genitalia in the female consists of a slitlike vulva and a small bump at the opening to the urethra.

Courtship

In captivity as well as in the wild, the rat's sense of smell plays a tremendous role in reproduction. Both sexes communicate not only their presence to one another but also their sexual receptivity or willingness to mate, through substances present in the urine and feces and on the skin. Male rats mark out territories by depositing drops of urine in areas where they roam. This marking behavior attracts females seeking to mate. It has been demonstrated that female rats prefer males they have mated with previously. Males do not exhibit this behavior.

Wild rats do not mature at the same rate as those born and raised in captivity. Wild female rats do not produce as many litters in their lifetime as their domestic and laboratory counterparts. This is likely due to environmental stress: climate, availability of food supplies, population density, disease, and predation. There is also variation in maturation and reproductive characteristics among strains of laboratory rats. The times for growth and gestation given in this text are averages compiled from several different sources. Your own breeding rats may not match up exactly.

To begin a rat colony, the novice breeder needs only a single pair of rats. Other breeding schemes call for one male to be housed with two to six females. Provided with enough space, the rats should get along with one another through the mating and gestation periods. More elaborate rotational schemes for breeding are used by research laboratories devoted to the production and maintenance of special strains of rats. These are less appropriate for the casual rat fancier.

The National Academy of Sciences has established guidelines for researchers working with rats. For instance, a single adolescent rat weighing about $3^1/_2$ ounces (100 gm) needs a minimum of 23 square inches (148 cm^2) of floor space. This is equivalent to a rectangle approximately 4 inches by 5 inches, which is very tiny indeed. In reality, you should provide a much larger habitat to give your pet an environment in which it can explore and move about comfortably.

Before placing two or more rats in the same breeding cage, give some attention to the size of the animals and the dimensions of the habitat. Housing rats in high density—that is, many animals in a small area—will dramatically influence their social behaviors: exploring, marking, feeding, gathering, fighting and reproduction. Cramped quarters adds great stress. The rats may fail to breed. Or they may fight among themselves or resort to cannibalism of the litter.

Mating

Rats bred in captivity begin to develop sexually at about 50 to 60 days (two months) of age. As with other mammals, this period in their life is defined as puberty. There is considerable variation between strains of rats as to the age at which male and female rats are actually fertile. Some rats begin to bear young as early as 65 days of age. Most rats become fertile a little later—at around 100 days (three months). By this time most rats weigh around 9 to 10 $^1/_2$ ounces (250–300 gm).

Once a female rat is capable of bearing young, she enters estrus (goes into heat) every four or five days. She is receptive to the male's advances for about 12 to 24 hours during the estrous cycle. Her mating behavior is controlled by fluctuations in sex hormone levels in her body, which in turn are influenced by environmental factors, such as overcrowding. Other physiologic factors, such as illness and nutritional status, also cause variations in the female rat's sexual response.

Unlike in the bitch, where the estrous cycle occurs on an average of only twice a year, unbred rats continue to have a four to five day estrous cycle over and over again throughout the year until she is pregnant. If a female rat is receptive to the male, she will arch her back and present her hindquarters to him and allow him to mount. After copulation, a waxy, whitish plug fills her vagina for about 24 hours. You may find this plug in the cage after it has been dispelled.

Gestation and Birth

Rats carry their young in the womb for 21 to 23 days. This is called the gestation period. You may leave a pregnant female in the habitat with the male or other pregnant females if you are using a harem breeding scheme, until around day 16 of gestation. But then she should be moved to her own quarters. This is recommended because males sometimes cannibalize

Delivery of the litter is usually uneventful. The mother licks and cleans each pup to remove the remnants of the fetal membranes, or amniotic sac that breaks during birth. This behavior stimulates the newborn to breathe and nurse, and bonds the offspring with the mother.

newborns, and because mothers do not nurse as well if they are left in the group.

Females build a nest out of the bedding material in which to give birth. Labor begins with the mother-to-be licking her vulva and the appearance of a clear vaginal discharge. The delivery takes about 1 $^1/_2$ hours. Litter size generally ranges from 6 to 12 pups, and each pup weighs approximately .2 ounce (6 gm) at birth. The pups are completely hairless, cannot see or hear, and are entirely dependent upon the mother for food and warmth. They even lack the ablility to urinate and defecate on their own; the mother stimulates a pup to do so by licking its perineum. You may be tempted to peek in and perhaps handle the newborn pups. Don't give in to this temptation, for disturbance of the nest may prompt the female to abandon or destroy the babies.

Reproduction and Breeding

Raising the Pups

Be sure that the nesting cage is not subjected to drafts, fluctuations in temperature or humidity, or excessive sunlight. Temperature should be between 70 and 80 degrees F and humidity between 40 and 70 percent. Do not use heat lamps or other high-intensity heat sources, which can make the temperature inside the cage rise dramatically, causing overheating and thermal burns. If the room in which you keep the cage is cooler than the recommended temperature and you must provide heat, use a hot-water bottle or a heating pad set on low and clothespinned to the side of the cage. Partially cover the cage to retain the heat.

It is possible to foster orphaned pups onto another female who is nursing a litter close in age. In the wild, female rats frequently share the responsiblity of raising the babies in a colony. Keep an eye on the foster mother to make sure she is eating and drinking and not becoming overburdened and weak. Also observe the foster babies to see that they have not been pushed out of the nest or cannibalized. A baby that is cold may be rejected, perhaps because the mother thinks it has died.

By ten days of age, hair covers the pup's body and the ears and eyes have opened. Mothers wean their babies at about 21 days. The pups now weigh about $1^1/2$ ounces (45 gm) with the males slightly heavier than the females. At this time, the young rats begin eating the rodent diet provided for the mother.

Female rats enter estrus again about 48 hours after delivery of a litter. It is possible to breed her again during this cycle. However, this puts an enormous strain on her body, since she now not only must support her own tissues and organs but must also produce sufficient milk for her babies while gestating another litter. If you wish to breed a female again, wait several weeks after weaning so her body has the opportunity to regain its strength.

Pregnant and nursing rats need the same type of nutrients that other females need: carbohydrates, proteins, fats, vitamins, and minerals. However, they need two or three times more of these nutrients, so they must eat more food. They also need more water while they are producing milk. Be sure to provide pregnant and nursing rats a fresh, well-balanced rodent diet at all times.

Under conditions of optimum husbandry, a female rat can produce a litter of offspring every month. Thankfully, this is not a realistic occurrence for rats in the wild, where variations in food supply, adequate shelter, and climate limit reproductive potential. Rat control officials tell us that a typical wild female gives birth to between three and seven litters every year.

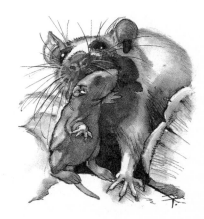

Mother rats require little assistance from you in caring for newborns.

31

Reproduction and Breeding

Rats are most fertile between three and ten months of age, after which the chances of conception at breeding and the number of pups per·litter begin to decline. Eventually, the female's ovaries fail to produce ova or eggs and the hormones that bring on estrus. This stage in the life cycle is called menopause and it begins at about 15 months.

Infertility

From the moment of conception, when the rat egg and sperm fuse and develop into an embryo, through to birth, many internal and external forces can cause the process to go awry. Infertility, miscarriages, resorption of embryos, failure of young to thrive, stillbirths, or birth defects can result. Aging, disease, inadequate nutrition, overcrowding, accidents, medications, and chemical exposure are examples of these forces. Breeding closely related animals can also cause problems. Some of these forces affect the developing embryo directly. Others cause mutations, which are changes in the genes themselves.

When a male and female rat are put together, offspring should soon follow. If this doesn't happen, first check to make sure you have a male and a female. Determining the sex of rats can be difficult when they're young, and mistakes are made even at pet stores. If this is not the problem, consider the age of your animals. Are they too young or too old? Also consider the habitat. Is there enough space for the animals to mate spontaneously?

It's a good idea to keep written records of when a male and female are put together and, if possible, of when they breed, so that the approximate delivery time can be calculated. If you have observed breeding behavior be-tween your rats but no pups have been delivered, the fetuses may be being resorbed during development. Be sure to note any unusual discharge appearing at the vulva of the female. Ask a veterinarian or scientist knowledgeable in laboratory animal reproduction to review your husbandry methods and the genetic background of your breeding stock.

Birth Defects

Mutations in genes can cause an organ or other body part to develop abnormally, and a birth defect sometimes called a "congenital defect" occurs. In a way, the word "defect" isn't a good one, because it implies that the abnormality is detrimental to the well-being of the animal. This isn't always so. Sometimes the "defect" gives an animal a survival advantage. If this trait is passed on through the offspring, eventually those members of a species that possess that advantage will outcompete and survive over the disadvantaged. (This is the basis for the theory of evolution or the "survival of the fittest.")

Scientists probably know more about the rat's genes than about those of any other warm-blooded animal. From this study we know that some out-of-the-ordinary occurrences at birth are really not so out-of-the-ordinary at all. Consider that some animals might be born with extra toes. Certainly we have all seen extra-toed cats. This trait is called "polydactyly" and it can occur in any species. It is generally not considered to be a problem to the animal and is quite charming in the cat. Fused toes, extra teats, absence of a tail or ears, sparse haircoat, no whiskers, these are examples of structure variation which would probably be of no consequence to the rat except that one might think that a bald rat would get chilly in the winter!

Some birth defects in rats are the result of outside influences, like drugs or chemicals, rather than mutations. A pup may be born highly underdeveloped or malformed, although this is rare. Some genetic defects might cause a physical difference that is not noticeable at birth but rather as the rat grows and can be compared with normally developing siblings. Spastic movements, circling, shaking, cataracts, and blindness may appear around the time of weaning. More than one problem can occur in a single animal.

Some of these genetic defects are very well-studied by scientists and geneticists. Strains of rats carrying these genes have been nurtured, because the diseases mimic similar disease and disorders in people. Scientists study the gene's effects in the hope of finding a way to eliminate them.

I was once presented with a young adult rat named "Stumpy." The reason for this moniker was obvious: she had no back legs to speak of, just two stumps in their place. Stumpy got around using her forelegs and these two stumps, which moved normally, since her hips worked just fine. When Stumpy was born, she nursed from her mother, grew fur, opened her eyes and thrived just as well as her other brothers and sisters. Stumpy's owner could no more think of destroying this creature for lack of legs than she could think of doing-in any of the "normal" siblings. So Stumpy lived on, and her mistress was careful to provide her with an extra soft surface in the habitat.

If you find yourself in the same situation as Stumpy's owner, of having to judge the quality of life of one of your young rats, consider carefully. If the rat eats, enjoys the companionship of its own kind, can move about without injury and is curious and inquisitive about its surroundings, then the choice for life is probably a good one. But if the rat is listless, uninterested in food or interaction, and is easily harmed or injured, your veterinarian can end its life humanely.

In a nutshell:
1. Average weight at birth: $^2/_{10}$ ounce (6 gm)
2. Number of pups in litter: 6–12
3. Age when body hair appears: 10 days
4. Age at weaning: 21 days
5. Average weight at weaning: $1^1/_2$ ounces (45 gm)
6. Age when puberty begins: 50–60 days
7. Age when breeding begins: 65–100 days
8. Age when most fertile: 3–10 months
9. Average weight when breeding begins: 9–$10^1/_2$ ounces (250–300 gm)
10. Frequency of estrous cycles: every 4–5 days
11. Length of estrous periods: 12–24 hours
12. Length of gestation: 21–23 days
13. Time for delivery of litter: $1^1/_2$ hours
14. Return to estrus after delivery: 48 hours
15. Average number of litters per year: 3–7 (up to 12)
16. Average age at menopause: 15 months
17. Average life span: 24–60 months

Nutrition and Feeding

Feeding Habits of Wild Rats

The success of rodents as a whole, and of rats in particular, can be largely attributed to their ability to adapt to a wide variety of circumstances, such as climate, harborage, population density, and food supply. A common rodent pet, the gerbil, lives naturally in the heat of the desert. The lemming, famous for its mass migrations, is found in the cold arctic tundra. Both of these species must find shelter from the temperature extremes, blowing winds, and glaring sun. They must search for seeds, nuts, and vegetation over land that supports the growth of very few plants.

Common brown and black rats found in nature have allied themselves with humans, living in and around buildings and dwellings, in sewers and drainpipes, in abandoned junk, and in waste-disposal sites. They are common among the docks and warehouses of harbor areas where water, shelter, and food is plentiful. Rat populations spread with people—as freeloaders in sailor's larders, for example. Where there are people, there are also rats.

At the north end of the Golden Gate Bridge in San Francisco is the fashionable town of Sausalito, a mecca for tourists. One warm and sunny Sunday, soon after moving to California, I was picnicking along the water's edge, sitting on the stone wall between the shop-lined Bridgeway Street and the harbor, with its bobbing houseboats. Halfway through lunch we were visited by several of the braver local harbor rats, who were scurrying and grappling among the rocks at our feet. I hoped they would be polite enough to wait for a leftover and not come up and take lunch right out of our hands. No doubt these rats had heard about the success their cousins the squirrels have at begging for food in Golden Gate Park across town!

The number of rats in any colony depends on the size of the habitat they have invaded, the amount of fresh water available, and, most important, the food supply. When food is scarce, the rats become more aggressive with one another. Some rats leave the colony to start a new one where there is more food.

Wild rats consume just about anything in order to survive. But, like most creatures, they eat what is easiest and most accessible first. I know of one very large rat colony established on a property in the country that borders on a freshwater reservoir. The rats have constructed a complicated labyrinth of burrows that extends from the edge of the reservoir underground to a nearby kennel, home to four wolf-dogs. At night, the rats emerge from their burrows and steal kibble while their unknowing benefactors sleep. Their forages are not always successful: Little One, the largest of the wolves, is an accomplished rat catcher. Nevertheless, these rats have done well for themselves. Some are as large as an average-size cat!

Rats do have food preferences, though. Rat-control officials have capitalized on these preferences in order to reduce the rat populations in human habitats. Brown rats are thought to have a preference for animal matter such as meat scraps. Black rats are thought to be primarily vegetarian. Rats prey on the carcasses of birds, cats, dogs, humans, and other rodents.

Two young solid rats. One sniffs the air inquisitively. ▶

Stories of aggressive rats attacking weak, debilitated, or even healthy animals are commonly passed on as truth and folklore.

Wild rats spend their nights scavenging for food. They eat seeds, nuts, berries, fruits, eggs from nests, and unprotected offspring of other animals and birds. They invade silos and bins to eat grains saved for planting or for feeding livestock. City rats scour cans and dumpsters for edible garbage and raid human dwellings for food. They leave behind damaged grain bags and containers, droppings, urine, and hair. If they are hungry, they may consume their plunder on the spot. But usually they carry or drag it back to the burrow before eating it. Rat-control officials take advantage of this behavioral tendency. Rat poisons are sometimes prepared into pellets that can be carried back to the burrow and shared with the rest of the colony.

Not all of the food that is brought into a rat nest is consumed. Some may go rancid, and will be eaten only if the supply of fresh food is limited. Rats that become ill but do not die from consuming rancid food or poisoned bait will shy away from the same foods later on. Your hungry pet rat is no exception; you should always provide fresh foods, lest it become finicky about its usual diet.

The National Academy of Sciences tells us that rats—or for that matter, all animals—have five basic nutritional requirements: energy, proteins, fats, vitamins and minerals. A defi-

Wild rats prefer to scavenge within a short distance of the nest. Remember this if your rat ever escapes from its habitat!

ciency in any single requirement will prevent all the others from performing their duties. Let's look at each requirement—what it is made of, its function, and how it is fulfilled in the diet.

Energy and Carbohydrates

Energy is derived primarily from carbohydrates, such as starches and sugars. Proteins and fats in the diet can also be metabolized into energy, but this is not their only function. The amount of energy contained in any food is measured in terms of calories. A calorie is simply the amount of heat that is given off when a substance is burned. In the laboratory scientists measure the calorie content of foods by burning a precise amount and then measuring the heat that is released in the process. Carbohydrates and proteins of all kinds produce the same amount of heat and thus have the same calorie contents. One gram of a

◀ Ramps, poles, and ladders added to the habitat keep your rats from becoming bored, and offer them a chance to exercise. By placing food rewards in unusual places, you encourage their natural scavenging behavior.

carbohydrate or protein contains four calories. Fats are far more concentrated bundles of energy; one gram of a fat contains nine calories of energy, more than twice that of carbohydrates and proteins. It is easy to see why people hoping to lose weight should avoid eating fatty foods!

Most of the rat's motivation for obtaining food comes from its need for energy. The amount of energy, and therefore calories, a rat needs depends on its life-cycle stage. Although rats never stop growing, they require more energy during their rapid-growth phase—from birth to approximately three to four months of age. After that time, their rate of growth slows and they don't need as many calories to sustain their tissues and provide energy for daily activity. That is of course, unless your rat is like my friend Kathy's rat, "Archey." Some years ago American River College, in Sacramento, California, held an annual Rat Decathalon. Archey distinguished himself at a young age by performing admirably in the maze events. Naturally, if your rat is also athletically inclined and gets a lot of exercise, it will need more calories each day than a rat with a more sedentary lifestyle.

Another of the rat's activities that requires energy is gestation and lactation of young. The mother eats to support her own body's needs and those of the pups developing inside the womb. The female rat increases her food consumption by 25 to 35 percent in order to meet those needs.

Energy is derived primarily from the carbohydrates found in grains such as oats, barley, wheat, milo, quinoa and rice. Vegetables like beans, corn, alfalfa, and peas contain carbohydrates in the form of starches and sugars, as do nuts and seeds. Inside the rats body, these foods are broken down and converted into a sugar called glucose, which is used for energy.

Without enough energy-producing foods, your rat will feel tired and lethargic. Energy-deprived young rats fail to grow; older animals lose weight and fail to reproduce. Severely energy-deprived animals may die from malnutrition or disease.

Proteins

Living creatures also require proteins in their diet. Proteins are long molecules made up of smaller ones, called amino acids, linked together. When protein-containing food is consumed, the links between these amino acids are broken down by the processes of chewing and digestion. The amino acids are then absorbed by the body and are used to rebuild the proteins into tissues, bones, nerves, hormones, blood, and other body fluids. Excess protein is used for energy or is stored as fat for later use.

Where do dietary proteins come from? From meat, of course.

Plant matter like grains, leguminous beans, corn, seeds, and nuts all contain proteins, too, because plants need proteins to form their tissues. No one plant contains proteins made up of a full complement of all the different kinds of amino acids needed by animals. People who are vegetarian must eat several different grains and beans in order to have a balanced diet. The same is true of the rat. The rat can get by just fine without meat, provided its vegetarian fare is made up of a variety of protein sources.

Without adequate protein in the diet, animals fail to grow, lose weight, and do not

Nutrition and Feeding

Principal Ingredients in the Diet

Ingredient	Function	Source	Amount needed	Signs of deficiency
Carbohydrates (starches and sugars)	Provide energy for daily activity, growth, and reproduction.	Grains, vegetables, seeds and nuts.	Approximately 75 percent of the diet, more in growing pregnant, and nursing animals.	Lack of activity, dull, not playful, weight loss or failure to grow and reproduce; death with severe starvation.
Proteins (amino acids)	Build body tissues: muscles, bones, nerves, hormones and blood, etc. Excess in diet is used for energy.	Meat, grains, seeds and nuts.	Minimum of 7 percent in adults, pregnant and growing animals need 15–20 percent.	Weight loss, hair loss, bone fractures, chronic infections, porphyrin-staining around eyes and nose, failure to grow and reproduce.
Fats (fatty acids)	Build body tissues and hormones. Excess in diet is used for energy or converted into fat stores.	Meat, nuts and seeds. The body makes some fatty acids on its own.	Very little.	Poor hair coat, scaly skin, failure to grow and reproduce. Unlikely to occur unless food is rancid.

reproduce just as if they were energy-deficient. More subtle signs of inadequate dietary protein are hair loss, stress fractures of bones, chronic infections, and porphyrin-staining around the eyes and nose (see In Sickness and In Health.) A minimum of 7 percent of the diet of mature rats should be protein. Rats under four months of age, pregnant females, and nursing mothers require more protein—about 15 to 20 percent.

Fats

Rats don't require much fat in their diet, but they do need some. Fats are very concentrated sources of energy. Gram per gram, fats provide more than twice the number of calories contained in either carbohydrates or proteins. Aside from being an excellent source of energy, fats function in the production of many hormones. They are essential components of tissue cells.

Excess fat is stored for later use when food is scarce. Body-fat stores are found inside the abdominal cavity surrounding the internal organs, inside the chest cavity surrounding the heart and great blood vessels, and in pockets under the skin and between layers of muscles. Excess fat puts pressure on organs like the heart and lungs, making it difficult for them to do their job. The added weight stresses the skeleton and makes for a slow and lumbering, clumsy animal. The extra wear and tear on joints can lead to early arthritis.

Just as proteins are larger molecules made up of smaller subunits, so are fats made up of small components. The components of fats are called fatty acids. Fatty acids are released from the fat molecule by the process of digestion, and are then absorbed into the body and put to work. Most of the fatty acids contained in foods can be manufactured by the body and need not be present in the diet at all. However, two or three fatty acids are essential—that is, it is essential that they come from a food source, because they can't be manufactured. Essential fatty acids are required in only trace amounts in the diet. But experts in rat nutrition tell us that rats grow better if there is about 5 percent fat in the diet.

Dietary fat comes from meat. It is fat that causes the "marbling effect" in roasts and steaks. Nuts and seeds also have a very high fat content. Rats, like humans, love the taste of fats in foods. Your rat may select out the peanuts and sunflower seeds from a mixture in its bowl. If allowed to eat a diet of mostly seeds and nuts, a rat will become fat and may develop deficiencies of other nutrients.

Because of the small amount required in the diet, a deficiency in the essential fatty acids is rather unlikely in a rat being fed an otherwise balanced diet. It is possible to have a fatty-acid-deficient diet—if, for example, food is stored improperly and goes rancid, destroying the fatty acids in the process. Rats deficient in fatty acids may exhibit poor hair coats, scaly skin, slow growth, or reproductive failure.

Vitamins and Minerals

Vitamins and minerals are also required in trace amounts in the diet. While glucose, amino acids, and fatty acids are the fuel and building blocks for energy and production of tissues, blood, and hormones, vitamins are required for those processes to take place. A newborn rat without vitamins in its diet is like a house builder with nails and wood but no hammer.

Vitamins

Scientists have given the vitamins names. The names describe chemical structures and are cumbersome to pronounce. So to make it easier to talk about them, some vitamins have also been assigned letter designations: A, D, C, E, K, and several called B. Vitamins D and C can be manufactured by the body itself (although this is not so in all animals; humans, guinea pigs, Old World monkeys, and some bats cannot). Vitamins A, E, and the B's must be included in the rat's diet. Bacteria that live in the intestinal tract make vitamin K, folic acid, and biotin.

To benefit from the bacterial synthesis of vitamins, rats, like some other animals, such as rabbits, practice coprophagy. A significant portion of the feces, about 50 percent, is eaten by the animal, and in this manner vitamins are recycled and conserved. This may sound like a thoroughly unpleasant prospect, but to the rat it is very necessary to survival. In addition, in times of food scarcity, nutritional deficiencies can be avoided or delayed by recycling substances that would otherwise be lost. Vitamins A, D, K, and E are recycled, and stored in limited amounts in the liver and fatty tissues of the body. Vitamin A, for instance, occurring naturally in carrots, causes quite a dramatic orange color to the skin when consumed in excessive amount.

Nutrition and Feeding

Principal Vitamins

Vitamin name	Its function	Signs of a Deficiency	Important in the rat's diet?
A	Necessary for healthy skin, eyes; growth and reproduction.	Scaly skin, blindness, failure to grow and reproduce, infections.	Yes
D	Necessary for healthy bones in adults and for growth in young animals.	Failure to grow, abnormal joints, soft bones, stiffness.	Yes
C	Helps make the substance that holds the body's cells together.	Wounds won't heal, failure to grow, bleeding.	No, the rat's body makes its own vitamin C.
E	Necessary to repair damaged cells and tissue; also needed for growth.	Failure to grow and reproduce, abnormal bone, muscle and heart tissue.	Yes
K	Blood clotting	Bleeding won't stop from even minor wounds.	Probably not*
B1 (thiamine)	Energy production from carbohydrates and proteins.	Deterioration of brain, nerves, heart and muscle tissue, loss of appetite, poor growth, weight loss.	Yes
B6	Many functions related to growth and energy.	Failure to grow and reproduce, poor skin and hair coat.	Yes
B12	Necessary for growth and for healthy blood.	Failure to grow, weakness, low fertility, death.	Yes, but deficiencies are rare.
Niacin	Many functions related to growth and energy.	Poor hair coat and skin, weight loss, porphyrin-stained whiskers.	Yes
Folic acid	Necessary for growth and healthy blood.	Poor growth, infections.	No*
Pantothenic acid	Many functions related to growth and energy.	Rough hair coat and flaky skin, graying of the hair, failure to grow and reproduce.	Yes
B2 (riboflavin)	Many functions related to growth and energy.	Unhealthy skin on face and legs, failure to grow and reproduce.	Yes
Choline	Works with folic acid and vitamin B12.	Liver and kidney damage.	Yes
Biotin	Necessary for healthy skin and hair; reproduction.	Hair loss, scaly skin.	No*

*This vitamin is made by bacteria that live in the intestines. Rats obtain it by eating their feces. This practice is called "coprophagy."

Nutrition and Feeding

Fruits, vegetables, nuts, and seeds are rich in minerals and vitamins and the ingredients, called "provitamins," that the body uses to make them. By providing your rat with a variety of these foods, you will ensure that it has a full complement of necessary vitamins and minerals. Pelleted feeds and grain mixtures available commercially contain all the vitamins in the necessary amounts, even those that the rat manufactures itself and those that are made by the rat's intestinal bacteria. Unfortunately, however, vitamins are subject to rapid destruction during storage and with exposure to heat and sunlight. Supplementing a commercial feed with fresh fruits and vegetables in small amounts can compensate for the loss in storage.

Vitamins and minerals are important to every one of a rat's body functions: growth and maintenance of skin, bones, nerves, eyes, and all other organs; blood clotting; wound healing; release of energy; muscle contraction; nerve impulse conduction; and excretion of wastes. They even help cells to hold their shape. The table on page 41 lists the known vitamins, along with their functions and deficiencies. Keep in mind that all vitamins work together and that there can't be a deficiency in one without there being a deficiency in others. Severe vitamin deficiencies are very unlikely in rats unless the diet is extremely restricted. Mild deficiencies are probably common. The deficiency signs listed in the table include those resulting from severely restricted diets. This information is included mainly for interest rather than for practical value.

Unkempt appearance, thin haircoat, scaly skin, stunted growth, all indicate a possible mild vitamin deficiency. However these signs are also seen with many diseases, such as mange or chronic pneumonia. Your veterinarian can examine your rat and review your husbandry practices to determine if your rat's diet is affecting its overall health.

Minerals

Minerals are involved in every process of the rat's body. Sodium and potassium are needed for electrical impulses to travel along nerves. Together with calcium, they allow muscles to contract. Calcium and phosphorus give strength to bones. Phosphorus also acts like a buffer that absorbs excess acids in the body. Your rat's body, as well as your own, uses iron to carry oxygen in the blood to tissues for metabolism. Sodium and chloride balance one another to help cells keep their shape. The mineral iodine is taken up by the thyroid gland and is incorporated into hormones. Other minerals—magnesium, copper, zinc, cobalt and manganese, for example—assist vitamins and proteins in a variety of processes necessary for life.

Most minerals are required in the diet only in very tiny amounts. The body has elaborate methods of conserving and recycling minerals using the kidneys. Some minerals are lost in stool and urine. That's why your rat produces a lot more urine if you feed it salty potato chips. Excess amounts of the minerals calcium, magnesium, and phosphorus in the urine can crystalize into bladder stones. This problem is much more common in other species of animals, such as dogs, cats and people but we can assume that rats have their fair share too.

Commercial rodent diets are supplemented with minerals, the chemical-sounding names listed at the end of the label or analysis over the bulk bin at the feed store. You do not need to add powdered vitamins or minerals to your rat's diet.

Basic Feeding Guidelines

A trip to your pet food store can be a bewildering and enlightening outing. On the shelves you will find a number of diets labeled for hamsters, gerbils, and guinea pigs, and an occasional package marked for mice and rats. Most give the impression that they are prepared with only one or two species in mind.

Commercial diets take several forms. A mixture of grains, nuts, and seeds may be coated with a vitamin and mineral supplement and sold as is. The same mixture may be ground and extruded to form pellets or larger lab blocks. These formulations tend to be less dusty. Unlike whole-grain mixtures, pelleted feeds are 100 percent nutritionally complete in each mouthful; your rat can't pick out its favorite ingredients and leave the rest.

Any of these rodent diets are suitable for the mature rat. The guaranteed analysis on the label usually gives the minimum percentages of crude protein and crude fats, and the maximum amounts of crude fiber, ash (minerals), and moisture (water) contained in the food. Remember that if the label says it contains a minimum of 5 percent fat, it may contain much more. If the grain feels greasy, it probably does.

The wholesomeness of a commercial diet is directly related not only to the quality of the ingredients it contains, but also to how it is prepared and stored. Any cooking during processing or storage under conditions of heat and humidity will cause loss of vitamin activity and rancidity of fats. Even under the best of circumstances, some deterioration of the diet's nutritional value is inevitable.

Most pet and feed stores sell rodent diets either in small, prepackaged quantities or in bulk, so you can purchase any amount that suits your needs. Slow turnover of inventory and less than optimal storage conditions at the distributor can leave the prepackaged diets nutritionally lacking and cannot be recommended. The prepackaged rodent diets are frequently more expensive than food sold from bulk bins as well. Mixed grains can cost more than pelleted feeds or lab blocks. Commercial diets run from $0.60 to $2.00 per pound, depending on the composition and packaging.

To be safe, buy only enough food to last for two months. After you bring the food home, transfer it to an air-tight container, and keep it in a cool, dry place. Monitor the food for freshness. There should be no smell or visible signs of mold.

You may come across some literature on small rodent care that suggests purchasing a variety of grains in 10- or 20-pound sacks and then mixing your own diets. But be careful of such suggestions. Unless you have a very large number of rats, homemade diets prepared in these quantities will probably lose their nutritional value before they can be consumed. For the average rat fancier with just a few animals, commercial diets make much more sense.

Use grains, pellets, or lab blocks as a food base. Supplement this base with a variety of fresh food from your table. Rats can eat virtually anything, but they shouldn't be fed potato chips or other foods high in fat and salt and devoid of any nutritional value. Dog kibble and cat crunchies are much too high in fat.

Chocolate contains a caffeinelike substance and is therefore unsuitable for rats. Most commercial rodent diets have inadequate protein levels for growing rats under four months of age and pregnant or nursing females. These rats should be fed diets supplemented with high-protein foods such as cooked meats, eggs, cheese, and nuts.

Wash all fruits and vegetables thoroughly before feeding them to your rat to remove hormone sprays and pesticides. Cut away all bruised or damaged portions. And do not offer your rat any moldy breads or produce. If you shouldn't eat it, your rat shouldn't either.

Pet store shelves are loaded with snacks, cakes, sticks, chews, crunchies, puffs, drops, and nibblets, all advertised as "treats" for your rat. A few are labeled as "gourmet blends," evidently for the discriminating rat. These foods are all combinations of the same ingredients found in a regular diet, although some have added molasses or fat-laden nuts, which make them very palatable to your rat's sweet tooth. These foods come in small packages at a premium price, but they are far less nutritious than a treat of dried or fresh fruits, crackers, nuts, cheese, or vegetables. They are a waste of money.

References used by scientific researchers specify that an adult rat will consume approximately 5 gm of food per 100 gm of body weight each day. Rapidly growing rats less than five months of age will eat twice as much. These numbers are not very useful, because a lot depends on variables such as how much exercise a rat gets, the weather, and the composition and palatablity of the diet. Feed your rat once a day. Put only as much food as will be consumed in a 24-hour period into the food bowl. Discard any leftover before refilling the bowl. Rats are mostly nocturnal feeders; that is, they eat at night. Alternatively, you can feed your rat exclusively by hand during its training exercises.

One last word on the use of vitamin supplements: Powdered vitamins and minerals can be purchased at animal supply displays. They are intended to be mixed into the rat's drinking water. This can lead to bacterial growth inside the containers, which in turn can cause diarrhea or dehydration, because the rat doesn't like the taste of the water and will not drink it. There is no need to add supplements of this type, if you are feeding your rat a well-balanced, high-quality diet.

Aside from hygiene, nutrition is the one factor you can control to ensure that your rat has a long and healthy life. The importance of a wholesome, well-balanced diet free of chemicals and additives cannot be overemphasized.

Feeding Your Sick Rat

Loss of appetite is one of the first signs that your rat is not feeling well. If this lasts for more than a day, you should take the rat to your veterinarian for a thorough physical examination. The veterinarian will prescribe any necessary medication and give instructions on nursing care. In addition, you may have to make a special effort to feed your rat until it is feeling better.

The most important thing you can provide for your sick rat is carbohydrates for energy. Take advantage of your rat's sweet tooth. Even water sweetened with table sugar, honey, or powdered fruit-flavored drink mix provides energy. Your rat may drink it eagerly from a dropper once you put the first drop into his mouth. But go easy with this; too much sugar will cause diarrhea. Sugar-coated cereals, and dried and fresh fruits like bananas are good choices.

I have had success getting some critically ill rats to eat instant oatmeal, especially the maple-brown sugar and apple-cinnamon-raisin flavors. Since these products have a pasty consistency, you have to add extra water to make them thin enough to pass through a dropper. You can also try baby cereal, grits, cream of wheat, cornmeal, or polenta. Make sure the cereal isn't too hot; room temperature or slightly above is best. It's easy to overdo it when you use a microwave oven.

Protein-rich foods like cooked eggs or baby food like strained meats (chicken, beef, veal, lamb) are easily lapped by an ailing rat. Even though your rat may not be eating much of its regular fare right now, leave some available in the habitat in case it gets the urge to nibble.

In a nutshell:

1. Purchase a small quantity of a balanced pelleted or mixed grain diet from your pet or feed store.
- Buy only what you will use in one to two months.
- Check for signs of mold or excessive dust.
- Feed purchased from bulk bins is best.

2. Store food in an air-tight dry container.

3. Fill the bowl once a day with fresh food. Offer only the amount your rat will eat in one day.

4. Wash and rinse the water bottle well and refill every day.

5. At least three times per week, offer table foods like vegetables, fresh or dried fruit, nuts, and cooked eggs.
- Wash and sort fresh fruits and vegetables thoroughly.
- Do not feed your rat spoiled produce.
- Do not feed your rat salty, fatty or caffeine-laced foods.

6. Vitamin and mineral supplements are unnecessary.

Training

A Most Appealing Fellow

One of the most appealing characteristics of domestic rats is their curiosity about—and their willingness to interact with—humans. Rats learn to trust their natural adversaries—cats, dogs, and humans—and sometimes even seek them out. The same cannot be said of the rat's more popular cousins, the guinea pig and hamster. These rodents have a much broader acceptance as pets because of their fluffy and colorful haircoats, teddy-bear appearance and soft oinks and squeaks.

Unlike their cousins, rats are far less likely to bite once they become accustomed to being handled. They are not as easily startled and are more accepting of human contact. They may become comfortable being turned on their backs or carried in a shirt pocket. Your rat may be only too willing to curl up and watch a movie with you, provided you share the popcorn.

Rats enjoy being petted. They particularly love being scratched under the chin and behind the ears.

Even in an unfamiliar environment, such as a veterinary hospital, a pet rat is unlikely to bite. Its first defense will be to urinate and defecate on its handler. Then it will make repeated and rapid attempts to free itself by wriggling and writhing. It may run for a familiar hiding place, like the shoe box you brought it in.

As a rule laboratory rats are different. These rats are under the stress of high-population density, which brings out aggressive tendencies such as biting. If you adopt a mature laboratory rat, you may find it to be less trusting. Most rats obtained as adolescents quickly respond to gentle handling.

Establishing Trust

Give your rat a day or two after arriving in your household to get over the stress of having been transported and to adjust to its new environment: the smell of the bedding and food, the habitat, room noises, lights. Once your rat has had the opportunity to explore its enclosure and mark it by urinating, and then eat and drink, it will be less frightened of being held. Spend at least 15 to 30 minutes each day interacting with your rat. Its acceptance of you will come more quickly if you feed it by hand, one small tidbit at a time.

Taking Advantage of Natural Behaviors

Food rewards have long been used by scientists studying behavior in rats. Circus and marine animal trainers do the same. Perhaps you have visited a marine park where sea mammals leap and retrieve floats for the favor

Training

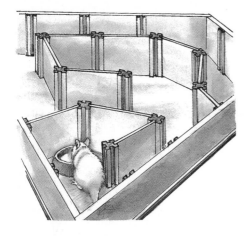

A rat will travel through a maze faster, after it has learned the pattern of turns it needs to take to reach the food reward at the end. A complex maze with many turns will take longer for a rat to learn. Not all rats learn maze patterns at the same rate.

of a fish. Trainers know that the tricks these animals perform are an extension of their natural behaviors. Dolphins, for instance, love to leap out of the water. Their trainers expand on this natural behavior by rewarding them when they leap in response to a signal. Because dolphins are innately intelligent, they put two and two together very quickly and so, learn to leap on command.

Of course a rat cannot learn to fetch your slippers or come when called. It can learn to retrieve or sit up if it is inclined to do so in its natural behavior. By observing its traits and postures and using food rewards along with signals, you can train your rat to perform certain "tricks" for you. My friend Richard has a rat named Splinter that will "fly" from its cage to the bed for a piece of peanut butter candy.

The most familiar example to all of us is a rat's ability to rapidly memorize the pattern of a maze. You can construct a maze at home. See how quickly your rat learns to navigate the course. Then redesign it and see how quickly your rat learns the new one. Compare these times with those of other rats, in an Ultimate Rat Race.

The best rat-in-a-maze story I ever heard came from my friend Denise. When Denise was a graduate student in psychology, she used Norway hooded rats in her experiments in perception. The rats were bred at the university and lived in a vivarium until it was time to use them in experiments. Denise would carry a certain rat in the pocket of her lab coat through the corridors to the laboratory. In the laboratory, rats were tested for their ability to recognize and perceive a subject, and were rewarded with sugar-sweetened water.

One rat, Mortimer, distinguished itself in these academic drills. Mortimer objected to being transported to the laboratory; he much preferred to travel there on his own. Denise would set him down on the floor and off he'd go, making the correct choice of left or right at each intersection along the way, with Denise following along behind him. Now who, may I ask, was training whom? Mortimer had learned the way to the laboratory from the trips there in Denise's pocket. And after he graduated from school summa cum laude, Mortimer lived out the rest of his days as her companion in Denise's office.

What Not to Expect

There are some things you cannot expect from your rat. Rats cannot be housebroken. Nor can they be trained not to chew furniture, electrical cords or anything else in their way for that matter. Except when put off by a strong smell or frightening sound, they explore anywhere they can. No matter how much you love your rat and think it is "bonded" to you, don't expect it to come to you on command. One rat admirer I know took her rat outside in the yard. Once on the ground with the land under its feet and the wind in its fur, it took off and was gone, never to be seen again. We can only hope it went and sought its fortune among its wild compatriots.

Rats cannot and should not be disciplined through physical force; to do so would be cruel and inhumane. Instead, training should consist of positive reinforcement of desired behavior.

In Sickness and in Health

Signs of Illness

Once you have spent some time with your rat, feeding, cleaning its habitat, playing, and perhaps doing some training, you will come to learn its unique behaviors. You will soon recognize its favorite foods, when and where it likes to sleep, its preferred places to be scratched, even its favorite places to explore while out of its enclosure. Behavior, appetite, and the color, consistency, and frequency of droppings and urine all reflect the general state of health of your rat. You should watch for labored or noisy breathing, discharge from the eyes or nose, sneezing, diarrhea, diminished appetite, changes in the amount or frequency of drinking, and unusual color or quantity of urine. Injuries or infection to the feet or limbs may cause your rat to limp or hold up a paw. A problem with the middle or inner ear may cause your rat to keep his head tilted to one side or to walk in a circle in one direction.

In this section, you will learn about the rat's internal organs and some of the diseases you may observe in your rat.

Skin

Did you know that the skin, or integument, is the largest organ system of the body? It is the first line of defense that rats and other living creatures have against disease and injury. The rat's skin and its adjoining structures—fur, nails, glands, whiskers, and lashes—all serve as a defense against predators and the elements.

The fur, or pelt, gives the rat insulation against cold and moisture. Sebaceous glands under the skin secrete oils that make the fur

Before beginning to groom itself, a rat often rises on its hindlegs and arches its back.

somewhat waterproof. These oils also contain chemicals that allow other rats to recognize each other. Tiny muscles in the skin attached to the hair shaft cause the hair to stand up higher, creating a thicker barrier, like the hairs on your arm when you have goose bumps. Fur also provides protection against bites from the long incisor teeth of other rats and predators. The agouti banding of the hair shaft is a neutral pattern that acts as camouflage for the wild-type rat.

Rats do not have sweat glands in their skin, except for the leathery pads on the bottoms of their feet. As a result of the excellent insulation provided by their coats, a rat easily becomes overheated. Toenails are used for climbing, grooming, defense, and for grasping objects. Whiskers on the face and scattered over the body are equipped with especially sensitive nerves that allow the rat to navigate through small spaces and along walls and crevices. Eyelashes sweep away debris to protect the surface of the eye.

Rats are very clean animals. They wash themselves from head to toe up to six times a day.

The skin, fur, nails, whiskers, and lashes are all affected by nutrition, infection, trauma, aging, parasites, and chemicals in the environment. And there are only a limited number of ways that the skin can respond to these influences. With the help of some simple diagnostic tests, your veterinarian may be able to find the answer to any skin problem your rat may have.

Hair loss, scratching, rubbing, chewing, swellings, scaling, and sores are all symptoms of diseases related to the skin. What follows are descriptions of the most common skin disorders found in rats.

Abscesses and Infections

An abscess is a warm, soft, and sometimes painful swelling under the skin. The skin over an abscess may become red, and the hair over an abscess can be easily pulled out at the roots, leaving a bald patch. An abscess contains accumulation of bacteria and pus cells under the skin. They are caused by germs introduced through a puncture or bite wound. Abscesses also occur spontaneously in old, debilitated,

and malnourished animals. When the pressure from the fluid under the skin is great enough, an abscess will rupture and drain. The fluid is milky, grayish green to yellow in color, and foul-smelling. Left untreated, an abscess may continue to fester and drain, or the infection can spread to other parts of the body. If you suspect that your rat has an abscess, apply a warm compress to the area using a wet cloth. Then call your veterinarian.

Lacerations

Cuts in the skin may be the a result of an accident while your rat was out roaming, or it may be the result of catching the skin on sharp wire on the cage. Lacerations less than an inch long and only skin deep usually heal without stitches if the wound is cleansed with a mild antiseptic soap and rinsed well with water. Try to prevent the affected area from becoming soiled and your rat from licking or chewing at it excessively. Watch for any signs of infection or abscessing.

Tumors

Tumors, both benign and malignant, are very common in rats. They can appear even at a young age. Tumors of the mammary glands, which lie in chains on both sides of the underbelly, are the most common tumors occurring in rats. They are usually benign. Benign tumors do not spread, but they may interfere with the function of other organs or limbs by taking up space, pushing normal tissues out of the way, or by leaving a rat unable to walk. Mammary tumors can grow to be very large. If not surgically removed, they often outgrow their blood supply, resulting in gangrene of the tumor itself. When this happens, toxic

Mammary tumors in rats are common and usually benign. These tumors may grow to be so large that they interfere with the rat's activities.

inciting an inflammation that can cause hair loss, greasiness, scaling, redness and severe itching. Rats will scratch, creating sores on their skin, especially in the areas behind the ears and along the back. Your veterinarian can diagnose mange by scraping the rat's skin with a small metal spatula or scalpel blade, putting the flakes of skin onto a clean glass slide along with a drop of oil, and looking for mites or mite eggs in the specimen with a microscope. Mange is frequently not curable, but it can be controlled with diluted pyrethrin-based shampoos and flea powders and through attention to nutrition and other underlying diseases. Mites do not live for long off an animal, and they are not contagious.

substances from the dying tumor are absorbed into the body, and the animal can become sick or die. Malignant tumors spread to other parts of the body, very often the lungs. This can cause difficulty breathing, loss of appetite, weight loss, lethargy, and, eventually, death. Any swelling or deformity should be examined by your veterinarian. Small malignant tumors can sometimes be removed before they have a chance to spread.

Mange

Mange is an infestation of the skin with mites. Mites are inhabitants of the skin and hair follicles found in all creatures. In young, healthy animals mites do no harm. In sick, old, debilitated, or poorly nourished animals, mites may flourish because of the immune system's inability to keep their numbers in check. Mites burrow through the skin, eating skin cells and

Ringworm

Ringworm is a fungal infection and does not involve a worm at all. The name of the disease refers to the circular or ring-shaped pattern of hair loss and redness created by the fungus as it grows in the skin. Several types of fungus cause ringworm, some of which are able to live in the soil as well as on animals. Ringworm is a contagious disease in humans and other animals. Should you see on your rat a ring-shaped lesion, hairless and scaly in the center, you should contact your veterinarian. Ringworm is usually not itchy.

Fleas

These tiny jumpers, flattened from side to side, do not confine themselves to dogs and cats. You may not observe live fleas on your rat, but rather their droppings, which they leave behind in the rat's fur and bedding. These droppings are little black flecks of dried blood that dissolve into a reddish brown liquid when they get wet. Should you observe fleas or their droppings, bathe your rat in a diluted pyrethrin-based flea shampoo safe for use on cats. Then contact your veterinarian for assistance in getting rid of these nuisances.

Lice

Lice are tiny, translucent, flat creatures that hold on to the hair shaft of the host. They cause intense itching and direct damage to the skin. Damage also results from the rat's furious scratching. Lice are not found on pet rats except under extremely unsanitary conditions and when there is contact with wild rats. Lice are species-specific; that is, they live on only one host. Your rat cannot give you its lice, and you cannot give it yours! The lice themselves are easily killed using a pyrethrin-based shampoo and flea powder, but the eggs, or "nits," are difficult to dislodge from the hair shaft. To fully solve the problem, attention should be given to correcting inadequate husbandry and sanitation practices, and to eliminating wild rodents from the premises.

Hair Loss

Loss of fur is not a disease in itself but a sign of some other problem. The problem may be any of a number of conditions, including infection, parasites, self-trauma, hormone imbalance, poor diet, or aging. Hair loss is usually accompanied by other signs such as scratching, sores, redness, or a discharge. If your rat shows signs of hair loss, have the rat examined by a veterinarian.

Torn Nails

Rats housed in wire mesh are subject to foot and nail injuries. At the time of the injury, torn nails may bleed profusely. The injured area can become contaminated with dirty bedding and feces. Left untreated, they may become infected, leading to lameness and even loss of toes or the entire foot. If an injury to the foot or nail occurs, apply pressure to the area with your fingers for 2 to 5 minutes until the bleeding stops. Wash sores on the feet with mild soap and rinse with water. Be sure to keep the bedding material clean. You may wish to change the floor surface in the habitat to one that offers more solid footing.

Ears, Eyes, Nose, and Lungs

The ears, eyes, and nose are sense organs. Besides providing the sense of hearing the ears play an important role in the sense of balance, which is extremely well-developed in the rat. Besides providing the sense of smell, the nose filters air entering the lungs of dust, germs, pollen, and other airborne particulates. Air passing through the nose is also warmed and humidified to protect delicate lung tissue from damaging dryness.

In the rat, constant tilting of the head, swaggered gait, reddish brown staining around the eyes or nose, face-rubbing, and sneezing are all signs of diseases that involve the upper respiratory tract, eyes, and ears. Wheezing, labored breathing, poor appetite, weight loss, and lethargy are indicative of problems involving the lungs. What follows are discussions of some of the more common diseases of these organs in the rat.

A healthy rat. The eyes and nostrils are free from any ▶ discharge. Note the shiny, smooth coat and pink skin on the ears and tail.

Ear Infections

Infections in the middle and inner ear behind the eardrum can cause a persistent tilting of the rat's head; uncoordination; and circling, rolling, or falling to one side. Treatment with antibiotics can reduce or eliminate these signs and prevent the infection from spreading. But in many cases the head tilting persists, usually because there has been permanant damage to the rat's sense of balance. This is usually a mild handicap, and the rat learns to compensate.

Conjunctivitis

Conjunctivitis is defined as an inflammation of the tissues surrounding the eye. It can occur when the rat's eyes are irritated by high ammonia concentrations inside cages, dust and chemicals in bedding, or detergent and disinfectant residues. It can also result from trauma to the eyes, or from reduced resistance to infection in old or sick animals. Conjunctivitis results in a discharge from the eyes, redness to the lids, hair loss, and face-rubbing. Excess tearing can cause sneezing. A reddish pigment produced by large glands behind the eye accumulates on the lids and nose. You may think this is blood, but it is not. These secretions are produced in excess during periods of stress and contain the same substances, called porphyrins, that turn blood red. Their presence

is a sign that your rat is under stress from illness, a nutritional deficiency, or a husbandry problem, even aging. If the irritation or infection is severe, it may spread to the eye itself causing the cornea to turn cloudy or bluish. Treatments for conjunctivitis include ointments and systemic antibiotics. Reduction of environmental stressors helps with therapy. Conjunctivitis is usually a recurrent problem.

Upper-respiratory Infections

This is probably the most common health problem in rats. Sneezing, porphyrin staining around the eyes and nose, wheezing, and labored breathing are all signs of upper-respiratory infections. Virtually all rats are infected early in life with a number of bacteria and viruses responsible for respiratory diseases. These germs live in harmony with the animal in the respiratory passages until certain conditions exist such as poor hygiene or nutrition, injury, illness, or lowered resistance to disease simply due to aging. For this reason, most rats show signs of respiratory disease by the time they reach one year of age. The illness can be controlled with antibiotics, but infection with the bacteria and viruses responsible for this problem cannot be completely eliminated except under strict laboratory conditions.

Pneumonia

Pneumonia is a frequent consequence of upper-respiratory infections in older rats. It usually results in severe debilitation and eventual death. Recoveries are possible with intense nursing care, strong antibiotics, and nutritional support. Signs of pneumonia are identical to the signs associated with lung tumors and irritation from heavy ammonia concentrations in cages. Your veterinarian can help you

◀ Two young rats engage in aggressive play behavior. The larger rat is of the hooded variety, the smaller has a wild-type pelt. Notice its lighter-colored underbelly. Both rats have agouti banding to the dark hairs.

to determine the best course of action in cases of suspected pneumonia.

The Heart and Circulation

The heart is a unique muscle whose function is to pump blood containing oxygen and nutrients throughout the body within a system of channels called arteries and veins. Like the rest of the body, these organs are subject to the effects of aging and stress. Aside from their general deterioration as an animal gets older, there are no specific diseases of the heart and circulation important to the pet rat.

Abdomen, Kidneys, and Reproductive Tract

A mammal's body is divided into two cavities by a muscular structure called the diaphragm. The thorax contains the heart and lungs. The abdomen, behind the diaphragm, contains the liver, stomach, intestines, kidneys, bladder, reproductive organs, and some important glands. In the abdomen, then, take place bodily processes vital to the digestion of food, assimilation of nutrients, excretion of wastes, conservation of water, and, reproduction.

Diseases in these organs cause diarrhea, weight loss, poor appetite, bloating, discharges from the birth canal, lethargy, and excessive water consumption and urination. Here are a few of these diseases of significance to the pet rat.

Diarrhea

Any change in color, frequency, or consistency of the rat's feces is considered to be diarrhea. Diet has the most significant effect on these characteristics. New foods and rapid changes in brands or types of diet are common

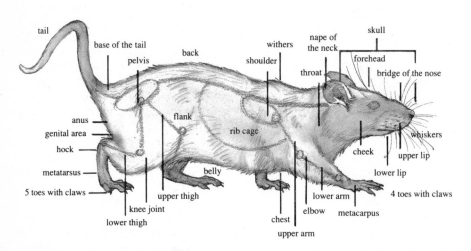

What is what on a rat. Knowing the names of the various parts of the rat is helpful, especially when talking to the veterinarian.

causes of diarrhea, especially if the rodent diet is old or stored improperly. Transient bouts of loose stools are usually of no consequence and resolve on their own, when the normal intestinal bacteria gets used to the new food. Persistent diarrhea, particularly when accompanied by weight loss, inactivity, poor appetite, or other signs of illness, can indicate a more serious problem, and a veterinarian should be consulted. Provide the veterinarian with a fresh stool sample for analysis for parasites. Tapeworms are occasionally responsible for diarrhea as well.

Kidney Disease

As rats get older, their kidneys lose the ability to cleanse the blood of waste products and conserve water. Rats compensate for this to some degree by drinking more water in an effort to flush out waste products through the remaining healthy kidney tissue. As a consequence, more urine is produced. This change in water consumption and urination may or may not be noticeable. Eventually, there is not enough healthy kidney tissue left to meet the body's requirement, and kidney failure occurs. Scientists have shown that diets high in protein will hasten the development of kidney disease. Once again we see how important nutrition is in determining health and longevity.

Bladder Infections

Cystitis, infection of the urinary bladder, is an infrequent occurrence in rats. When it does occur, it usually causes blood in the urine. Cystitis can be treated successfully with antibiotics, although it is sometimes complicated by the presence of bladder stones or tumors which can be palpated by a veterinarian.

Muscles and Bones

Bones connect to form a skeleton. Attached to the skeleton are the muscles. Together, muscles and bones provide protection for the internal organs and allow for locomotion. Did you also know that there are bones in the ear and muscles in the intestines? Limping, holding up of a paw, and abnormal angles to limbs indicate diseases of bones and muscles. These diseases are usually the result of some trauma. They are also painful; your rat may try to bite you if you examine it. Minor muscle soreness, sprains, and strains usually disappear in a day or two if the rat rests. Persistent lameness indicates a possible broken bone and should be investigated by your veterinarian.

Nervous System

Nerve tissues carry chemical impulses throughout the body, directing all the other organs in their physiologic functions. This is somewhat analogous to electrical lines carrying power to homes and businesses, with the brain and spinal cord as the power plant. Nerve tissue is subject to the same effects of nutrition, chemicals, aging, and trauma as all other tissue on the body. In rats, aging and trauma have the greatest effect on the nervous system.

Diseases of the nervous system manifest themselves in the rat as uncoordination, trembling, seizures, paralysis, and depression.

Chemical Poisoning

Accidental poisoning can occur while your rat is outside its cage unsupervised. For example a rat may ingest a household chemical while chewing through a plastic bottle or cardboard container. Muscle tremors, uncoordination, collapse, seizures, or hemorrhage may result. The rat's small size makes onset of symptoms rapid, and little can be done to prevent death in most instances. The same signs can occur in cases of overdose from, or exposure to, pest-control products, applied either to the animal or the environment. Wash the rat off with mild soap and clear water as soon as possible to prevent further absorption of the products through the skin. Your veterinarian can perhaps administer an appropriate antidote.

Seizures

Collapse, paddling of the feet, gasping, sudden and simultaneous release of urine and feces, and unresponsiveness are all signs of a seizure. Seizures can result from poisoning, head trauma, tumors and infections in the brain, and degenerative changes associated with aging.

Degenerative Myelopathy

Aging rats, most frequently those over two years, may become uncoordinated or paralyzed, particularly in the rear legs. This may be due to degenerative myelopathy of nerves that carry impulses to the muscles of the limbs. It is not a fatal disease; however, it can be very debilitating in its later stages. The animal may be unable to move around the cage well, and eventually may not be able to reach food or water. Outside its habitat, the rat is at greater risk of injury from falls and aggression from other animals. Calluses and sores may develop on the knees from crawling. As with other illnesses associated with aging, your veterinarian can help you assess your rat's quality of life.

Miscellaneous Diseases

Ringtail

If relative humidity is consistently less than 40 percent in its environment, a young rat may develop annular or ringlike sores around the tail on one or more locations. In severe cases, the end of the tail may fail off, leaving a stump. In other instances, the sores will heal, resulting in a constriction at this site. This condition is commonly found in one- to two-week-old domestic rats born during the winter months, when indoor air is usually very dry. It is also more commonly found in rats housed in cages. Nothing can be done to correct the problem once it occurs. Changing to an aquarium habitat may raise the relative humidity in the rat's environment enough to prevent subsequent litters from being affected. If you are using processed corncob for bedding and this problem occurs change to wood shavings or a cellulose product.

Overgrown Teeth

The rat's four front teeth, or incisors, grow continuously—at a rate of about 4 to 5 inches a year. They require constant grinding to keep them at a functional length. This is done through the rat's natural gnawing behavior. If the upper and lower incisors are not properly opposed to one another, normal wearing cannot occur and the teeth will eventually curve to the side or penetrate the roof of the mouth or under the tongue. This condition, called a malocclusion, occurs if either the upper or lower jaw is too short or too long. Rats with a malocclusion should not be used for breeding, because this harmful trait is passed to the offspring. Overgrown teeth must be trimmed periodically to

Quick Reference to Diseases of Rats

Symptom	Body system	Possible cause	What to do
Hair loss	Skin and fur	External parasites, nutrition, old age, self-trauma	Consult your veterinarian
Scratching, chewing, rubbing (self-trauma)	Skin and fur	External parasites, infections, chemical irritation (e.g., soaps and disinfectants, chemicals in wood shavings)	Consult your veterinarian, remove any known irritant, bathe in clear, fresh water
Swelling, sores, scaly skin	Skin and fur	Infections, abscesses, tumors, nutrition	Consult your veterinarian
Bleeding	Skin, urinary tract	Self-trauma, cuts, injuries and accidents, fighting, see "blood in urine"	For wounds, use clean cloth and apply pressure to stop bleeding, consult your veterinarian
Limping, holding up one leg or paw, loss of tail tip in infant rats	Muscles, tendons, ligaments and bones	Injuries and accidents, fighting, broken bones, low humidity in the nursery	Consult your veterinarian, raise relative humidity to over 40 percent
Sneezing, brownish red discharge around eyes and nostrils	Eyes, nose, sinuses	Infections with viruses or bacteria, nutrition	Consult your veterinarian
Deep, labored breathing, lack of energy	Lungs	Bacterial or viral pneumonia, cancer	Separate from other animals, keep warm, do not handle unless necessary, consult your veterinarian
Diarrhea	Intestines	Internal parasites, changes in diet, infections	Keep diet constant and simple, consult your veterinarian
Blood in urine	Kidneys and bladder	Infections, stones, cancer	Consult your veterinarian
Tilting of the head, circling, stumbling, falling over, dragging the hindquarters, seizures	Ear, brain and spinal cord	Infections, poisons, accidents (falling), and injuries, nutrition, old age	Confine to habitat to prevent injury, remove known poisons, consult your veterinarian
Weight loss, lack of appetite	Many, look for other signs of illness	Overgrown teeth, infections, cancer, old age	Consult your veterinarian, offer fresh food

allow the rat to eat and to prevent sores in the mouth. This is easily accomplished using a nail trimmer. (See "Trimming teeth," page 62.)

Basic Nursing Care

The same basic principles of first aid that are used on larger companion animals and humans also apply to the nursing of sick and injured rodents. The rat's small size and intolerance of devices such as bandages and splints are obstacles to their care. With patience, agility, and a little common sense, you can assist your rat in its recovery.

If your rat has fallen, become trapped by a door or a drawer, been stepped on, swatted by the dog, or strafed by the cat, be sure to isolate it quietly in its cage for observation. Apply direct pressure to any bleeding cuts to stop the

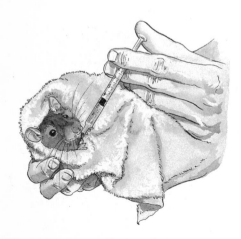

When giving your rat medication, offer it a drop from the syringe or dropper. Restraint may be unnecessary, but most rats need to be wrapped in a towel and "scruffed."

hemorrhage, but otherwise the rat should be left alone to recover from the trauma. If bleeding, lameness, breathing difficulty, depression, or pain persists, call your veterinarian. A fracture or internal injury may have occurred. Do not attempt to apply bandages or splints yourself. Improper application can result in a cutoff of circulation and subsequent loss of the limb.

The veterinarian may prescribe medication to be administered into the rat's eyes or mouth, or into the drinking water. You may be instructed to clean and treat wounds, give therapeutic baths, observe surgical wounds for infection, or other special treatments. Make sure you fully understand the doctor's instructions, and don't hesitate to ask for a demonstration or tips on restraining your rat for these procedures. Many are described below.

Many of the commonly used antibiotics used on rodents are palatable to rats, so oral medications are usually not a problem for owners who have rats that are used to being handled. However, ointments and a few of the procedures can be frightening or uncomfortable for the rat, and it may struggle. You can safely immobilize a rat by "scruffing" it (this is described under "How to Pick Up a Rat, page 24) or by rolling the rat in a hand towel and leaving its head exposed.

Oral Medication

Liquid medicine is administered in drops from a dispensing bottle, medicine dropper, or syringe. If possible, have the appropriate aliquot prepared in the dropper or syringe before the rat is in your hand so you don't have to fumble and risk spilling it. Hold the drop at your rat's lips and it will probably lick each one offered. Follow all instructions for mixing and storage of the medicine.

Medicine in Drinking Water

Ordinarily, this is not the best way to administer medication to sick animals, rats or otherwise. Oftentimes, the medicine doesn't taste good to the rat, so the rat may decrease the amount of water it usually drinks or refuse to drink at all. That means that your patient doesn't take its medicine or won't receive an adequate dose. Inadequate water intake also means the rat might get dehydrated and get even sicker than before.

On the other hand, if you have to medicate a lot of rats at one time for a chronic infection like an upper-respiratory disease, putting medication in the water may be the most efficient course. Medicated water should be prepared fresh every day. Be sure to ask your veterinarian if the solution remains stable when exposed to light. If not, wrap the bottle tightly in aluminum foil.

The rats may be more likely to drink medicated water if you sweeten it with a little sugar or fruit-flavored powdered drink mix. Your veterinarian can instruct you as to the amount of water you should use to dissolve the powder. If you are given capsules, you will have more success if you open the capsules, dissolve its contents in water, and discard the capsule itself. Tablets can be crushed to a fine powder between two spoons or with a mortar and pestle.

If you can't get the powder to dissolve or if flakes reappear after the bottle sits undisturbed for a while, contact your veterinarian. This could mean that there is bacterial growth inside the bottle or that a chemical reaction is occurring with some other substance. The medicated water should be your rat's only source of water during treatments. Again, *be sure your rats are actually drinking the water* so that they don't become dehydrated.

Eye Ointments

With your rat wrapped safely in a towel, squeeze a small amount of ointment across its eyes. Gently open and shut the lids to distribute the medication across the cornea.

Compresses

Run a clean cloth or stack of gauze pads under very warm running water and wring out most of the moisture. The temperature of the compress should be comfortable to the touch.

Apply ointments directly across the rat's eye and distribute them by gently opening and closing the lids.

Hold the compress firmly over the area to be treated until it cools. Repeat this procedure for the time period suggested by your veterinarian, usually five to ten minutes.

Caring for Bandages and Splints

Bandages and splints are applied to limbs in a way that leaves the rat's toes exposed. These devices can slip down once the rat becomes more active, which can compromise their effectiveness. Watch to make sure that the rat's toes don't swell or change color from pink to blue to black. Keep bandages clean and dry by changing the bedding frequently.

Caring for Postsurgical Wounds

Watch the incision for signs of redness and swelling. Some of this is normal and indicates that healing is taking place. If a puffy area appears painful or oozes a foul-smelling discharge, call your veterinarian.

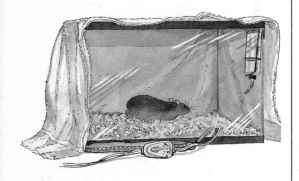

To set up an incubator, place the aquarium half on and half off a heating pad. Your rat can then choose to lie on either a warm surface or cooler surface, depending on its preference. Never turn the temperature setting higher than low.

Setting up an Incubator

Seriously ill animals can benefit from raising the temperature in their environment a few degrees. This is easily accomplished by placing a heating pad under the habitat. Set the pad's thermostat on low and put a towel between the pad and the cage or aquarium to prevent the temperature inside from becoming too high. If you house your rat in a cage, place another towel over most of the cage to retain the heat, or fasten the heating pad to the side of the cage with clothespins and then cover the cage with a towel.

Trimming Teeth

Get instructions from your veterinarian prior to trimming your rat's overgrown teeth to prevent accidentally trimming the teeth too short. Wrap your rat in a hand towel, leaving the animal's head exposed. Using a folding nail trimmer, snip the curved overgrown section of the upper and lower incisors to the length of approximately $^1/_2$ inch (1 cm). Incisor teeth in large rats can be trimmed using a Resco-type dog-nail trimmer. Simply slip the arched bar into the mouth and around the tooth and briskly close the handle. File any sharp edges with a nail file.

Trimming Nails

Examine your rat's nails for the pink center, or "quick," containing sensitive tissue and capillaries. The quick will bleed if you cut the

A mother rat and her babies. She is alert for any danger. ▶
These four babies will be weaned to solid food as soon as this family has outgrown the nest.

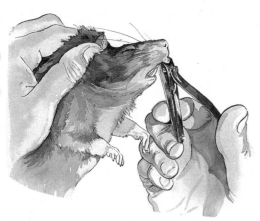

The keys to safe teeth trimming are: adequate restraint and a sharp tool.

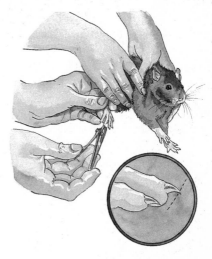

It is easier to trim the tips off sharp claws if one person holds your rat and the other person holds the toe and trims.

nail too short. Use a folding trimmer to remove just the sharp points of the nails. If bleeding occurs, apply pressure to the end of the nail. Then quickly release the pressure and apply a pinch of silver nitrate (Qwik Stop) powder or flour to the momentarily dry tip.

Bathing

Pyrethrin-containing flea shampoos for cats are used to control mange in older rats. Follow the instructions on the bottle for length of application. With plenty of clear warm water, rinse away all irritating soap residues, being careful to avoid getting soap and water in the

rat's ears and eyes. Then towel dry the rat and finish the job with a hand-held hair dryer. Hold the dryer at least a foot away from the rat to prevent burns, and be careful not to blow warm air directly into the rat's eyes.

Diseases People Get From Domestic Rats

Earlier, we talked about diseases wild rats transmit to humans through direct contact and through contamination of food and water with droppings and urine. Diseases that animals transmit to people are called *zoonoses*. For the most part, zoonotic diseases of wild rats do not occur in laboratory or commercially bred rats except in the unlikely event that a breeding facility has been unknowingly harboring wild rats. But there are a few potential problems that rat fanciers should know about.

◄ A young rat sharpens its balancing skill. Off he tumbles, only to try again! The inner and middle ear control the sense of balance which will improve with practice.

In Sickness and in Health

The most common problems researchers and people working with domestic rats encounter are allergic reactions to rat dander and hair, and injury or infection secondary to rat bites. The incidence of these problems is unknown, because they are not required by law to be reported to disease-control centers. Laboratory rats are known to carry organisms such as *Leptospira, Salmonella,* and *Pneumocystis carnii* with significant frequency. These organisms pose little or no threat to healthy people, but they *can* pose a threat to people whose immune systems are not working well.

The Geriatric Rat

Pregnancy in rats lasts for 21 to 23 days. Babies nurse from their mothers for about three weeks. Puberty begins at about 50 to 60 days of age, and by 100 days of age, successful mating can occur. Female rats are capable of producing young until they are about a year and a half old. By 18 months, rats of both sexes begin to develop changes in their internal organs, muscles, nerves, and bones related to old age. By the time it is two years old a rat is considered old. Despite the changes occurring inside their bodies, many pet rats can live to the age of three, four, or even five years, although that is rare. When you consider that every ten days of a rat's life is equivalent to one year of human life, a two-year-old rat is the same age as a 73-year-old person!

Rats have been used for decades in research on nutrition, cancer, heart disease, obesity, learning, toxicology, aging, and just about every other branch of biological science. Because of this research, much is known about aging in rats—what goes on at the level of the cell, the organ, and ultimately the whole body. A rat's aging depends on many complex interactions among genetics, nutrition, reproduction, and environmental conditions. No single factor determines whether your rat lives a long time. Attention to all these factors will optimize the chances of having a healthy, happy pet.

As your rat gets older, you may begin to notice changes in its behavior and overall body condition related to the aging process. The most common diseases of geriatric rats include tumors or cancer, chronic respiratory disease (especially pneumonia), kidney disease, and nerve deterioration. These conditions are discussed in detail under "Signs of Illness," (beginning on page 49). They are usually accompanied by an increase or decrease in water and food consumption, difficulty in breathing and walking, lethargy, and loss of weight.

The signs of aging in rats do not appear suddenly overnight, but come on gradually and often without immediate notice. The rat's body has a remarkable capacity to adapt. So despite the presence of a swelling under its foreleg or a discharge from its nostrils, your rat's quality of life may be quite good.

Unlike with humans and even other companion animals like dogs and cats, there is not a lot that can be done to cure some of the diseases in older rats. Diabetic dogs can be given insulin injections; kidney disease can be controlled with fluid therapy and medication. These measures are impractical if not impossible to do to a $10^1/_2$ ounce (300 gm) rat. However, external tumors can be removed, especially if they are small. This may not lengthen the life of your rat, but it may improve the quality of its life. Your veterinarian can help you decide if a surgical procedure is appropriate.

What should you do for your rat to minimize handicaps and maximize its enjoyment of life? First, be sure to practice good hygiene and housekeeping. Offer foods that you know are favorites of your rat. Be sure to use prescription medications exactly as instructed by your veterinarian. Supervise your rat's playtime, especially if it has difficulty walking, to prevent injury.

When Euthanasia Is Necessary

No matter how small and insignificant or undesirable rats may seem to some people, they do come to share our lives, perhaps as much as any other companion animal. We form bonds and attachments with them when we care for them and learn to recognize the differences in personalities from one rat to another. So at the end of their life, the loss of your rat can cause you as much grief as the death of any other pet.

Most people abhor taking an active part in the death of an animal and this includes making the decision when to end a life for humane reasons. We would rather that old and sick pets simply not wake up from sleep one morning, freeing us from the responsibility of deciding that the time has come to end its suffering. Unfortunately, this rarely happens and we are sometimes forced to recognize that we must assist an animal to die.

We are fortunate in veterinary medicine, to be able to end the suffering of animals, despite the grief it causes for those left behind. Your veterinarian can help you to come to this decision; not every circumstance is the same. By understanding the arguments pro and con, the sadness will be easier to bear.

Euthanasia, or mercy killing, is very nearly painless. Most veterinarians perform this procedure by administering an overdose injection of an anesthetic. The animal simply goes to sleep, and its breathing and heart activity stop. The only pain involved is the prick of a needle.

Glossary

agouti. Type of banded coloring to the hair shaft that provides camouflage for many animals.

aliquot. Carefully measured amount of a substance, usually a liquid.

annular. Shaped like a ring.

anus. Opening of the gastrointestinal tract where feces or stool exit the body.

bubonic plague. A disease caused by the bacteria *Yersinia pestis* and transmitted to humans by the bite of rat fleas.

calorie. Unit of heat given off by a specific amount of a food when it is burned in a laboratory experiment.

cannibalism. The act of eating a member of one's own kind for food, ritual or out of aggression.

carnivore. Animal that eats meat exclusively.

cataract. In the rat's eye, a cloudy defect located inside the lens that prevents the passage of light through the eye to the retina.

chromosomes. Group of genes.

commensal. Living together.

congenital. Present at birth.

coprophagy. Practice of eating excrement or feces.

copulation. Act of mating; a male and female come together to join the sperm and egg that produce offspring.

cornea. Transparent surface on the front of the eye through which light passes.

diastema. Space between the upper and lower jaws of rodents behind the incisors and in front of the molar teeth.

estrus. Period during reproduction when a female will allow a male to mate and conception takes place.

external genitalia. Reproductive organs located on the outside of the body.

extrude. To push through.

euthanasia. To kill an animal in order to relieve its suffering; sometimes called "putting an animal to sleep."

feces. Solid waste material from the body; stool; excrement.

gene: A piece of DNA information inside a cell.

genital papilla. In female rats, the small bumplike opening of the urinary tract.

geriatric. Aging or old.

gestation. Process of development and growth of young inside the uterus or womb. Gestation time refers to the length of time for this process to occur. It differs for every kind of animal.

harbinger. Carrier or bearer.

harborage. Place to live.

humidity. Amount of moisture in the air.

hybrid vigor. Refers to the health and vitality often possessed by outbred animals.

hypothermia. Low body temperature.

inbred. Animals that are closely related to one another and have almost identical information on their genes.

incisors. In rodents, the four large front teeth used for gnawing.

integument. Skin.

Glossary

iris. Colored part of the eye that surrounds and regulates the size of the pupil and the amount of light that reaches the retina.

labyrinth. A maze.

lactating. Nursing.

leptospirosis. Disease caused by various bacteria called *Leptospira*, transmitted in the urine of rats.

lethargy. Lack of energy.

longevity. Lifespan.

mammals. Group of warm-blooded animals that have backbones, bear live young, and nurse the young from mammary glands.

menopause. Stage in the life cycle when a female can no longer conceive and bear young.

molars. Grinding teeth in the back of the mouth; not visible in the live rat.

mutation. A spontaneous change in the information carried on a gene.

omnivore. Animal that eats meat, plants and decaying matter.

outbred. Animals that are not closely related to one another and have very different information on their genes.

palpate. To feel an organ or limb for its size, shape, consistency, and mobility to learn if it is injured or diseased.

pathogen. Germ or microorganism that causes disease.

perineum. Area of the rat's body under the tail that includes the skin surrounding the anus, scrotum and genital papilla.

phenotype. Any characteristic of an animal that is decided by the information on a gene.

polydactyly. The condition of having extra toes or digits present on a hand or paw.

polygamous. Term to describe animals that mate with more than one other animal of their own kind during their lifetime.

porphyrin. Substance contained in blood, saliva, and tears that turns reddish brown when exposed to air and light.

predation. Act of hunting and killing prey (other animals) for food.

prolific. Term used to describe animals that reproduce quickly and have many offspring at one time.

puberty. Stage in the life cycle when reproductive organs and sexual behaviors develop and mature.

pupil. Hole in the iris through which light passes to the retina.

pyrethrin. Insecticide purified from the chrysanthemum flower.

rancid. Rotten or decayed.

retina. Tissue lining the back of the eye that receives light and transmits it as nerve impulses to the brain to create a visual image.

rodents. Largest group of mammals, composed of animals having a space called a diastema behind continuously growing incisor teeth.

scrotum. Sac of skin that contains the testicles.

sebaceous glands. Oil-secreting glands associated with hair follicles

tactile. Refers to the sensation of touch.

Glossary

testicles. In males, the organs responsible for making sperm and the hormones necessary for reproduction.

toxicology. Study of toxic or poisonous substances.

transmissible. Able to be passed on from one animal to another.

urethra. Opening in the genital papilla where urine exits the body.

vagina. Canal through which the newborn passes from the uterus to the outside world during birth.

vivarium. Habitat in which animals are raised in captivity as close to natural conditions as possible.

vulva. Opening of the birth canal where the young emerge from the female.

Yersinia pestis. The bacteria that causes bubonic plague.

zoologist. Scientist who studies animals.

zoonoses. Diseases that are transmitted between humans and animals.

Index

Index